SPELLBOUND

For Anne,

with the best wishes

and regards of the

author

[signature]

March- 2013.

SPELLBOUND

Friends of John Keats

Peter Davey

Pen Press

See the acknowledgements for the works
and books of authors referred
to and quoted from within this work.

The publisher bears no responsibility
for the accuracy of information recorded within this book

ISBN: 978-1-78003-482-9

First published in Great Britain by Pen Press
All paper used in the printing of this book has been made from
wood grown in managed, sustainable forests.

Printed and bound in the UK
Pen Press is an imprint of
Indepenpress Publishing Limited
25 Eastern Place
Brighton
BN2 1GJ

A catalogue record of this book is available from
the British Library

By the same author:
Thorns and Ivy – 2001
Tommy – 2002
A Poet in Love – 2009
Zetsubo – 2011

Cover design by Jacqueline Abromeit

Dedication

This book is dedicated to the memory of

Kohji Aoyama

The celebrated Japanese author and fellow Keatsian

Mr Kohji Aoyama – At the Protestant Cemetery, Rome.

Acknowledgements

Without those who have researched, studied and written about John Keats before me, this book would never have come into being. Their work, along with my own research and feeling for the poet, has inspired me over the time it has taken to write this book.

I therefore owe a debt of gratitude to all who have trodden this path before me, and I have leant most heavily upon the following works:

Robert Gittings' *John Keats – The Living Year* – 1954 and *Keats* – 1968

Maurice Buxton Forman's *The Letters of John Keats* – 1935

John Middleton Murry's *The Poems and Verses of John Keats* – 1949 and *Recollections of Writers – Charles and Mary Cowden Clarke* – 1878 (Reprint 1969 – Centaur Press Ltd)

Joanna Richardson's *The Everlasting Spell* – 1963

General facts and information from – *Nelson's Encyclopaedia* (1963 edition)

I also wish to thank those who have supported me and given practical help during the period of my study. It was the Japanese author of *Keats My Genius* – 1998 Kohji Aoyama, (now deceased) who set me upon this road.

My fellow members of the Suffolk Poetry Society, who gave up valuable time to read and advise on the manuscript, Judy Ryland who read 'Charles Cowden Clarke and Charles Armitage-Brown', and Frank Wood, 'Joseph Severn'. My computer-literate friend, Mr Brian Peters for his transmutation of my W.P. disks to Microsoft Word format.

Mari, my wife, for her artwork. The London Metropolitan Archives for permission to reproduce images from the collection in Keats House, Hampstead. The National Portrait Gallery for the portraits of John Keats by Joseph Severn and Charles Cowden Clarke by an unknown artist.

And for his help with the research into Wentworth Place, I should like to thank Mr Kenneth Page, the information officer at Keats House.

Contents

Information on the illustrations

John Keats – From a miniature by Joseph Severn, 1819 (*page no.* 89)
(National Portrait Gallery, London.)

Charles Cowden Clarke – 1787–1877 (*page no.* 90)
From a painting by an unknown artist. (National Portrait Gallery, London)

Charles Armitage-Brown – 1787–1842 (*page no.* 91)
Photograph of the bust, the only likeness of 'Keats' 'capital friend'.
Made in Florence in 1828 by the sculptor Andrew Wilson.
(From the collection at Keats House, Hampstead)

Joseph Severn –1793–1878 (*page no.* 92)
From a self portrait aged 29.(Keats House, Hampstead)

The Clarke's School, Enfield (*page no.* 93)
Keats and his brothers, George and Tom, were educated there. Keats from 1803 to 1811. A fine three-storeyed building in red brick, built 1717. In 1849 it became the Station House for Enfield on the Eastern Counties Railway line. Demolished in 1872, with part of the front elevation preserved within the Victoria and Albert Museum.
(From an impression in watercolour by Mari Davey 2012)

Doctor Hammond's House, 'Wilston', 7 Church Street, Edmonton (*page no.* 94)
Where Keats served his apprenticeship for the medical profession, living in over a period of four years, 1811 to 1815. Demolished in 1931 to make way for a line of shops.
(From a watercolour by Mari Davey 2010)

Continued...

Wentworth Place (Keats House),
Keats Grove, Hampstead, London (*page no.* 95)
Built by Charles Armitage-Brown and Charles Wentworth
Dilke in 1815. Here Keats first met Francis (Fanny) Brawne
in Oct/Nov 1818. Keats lodged here with Brown in his part
of the house. Fanny and her mother nursed the ailing Keats
in Dilke's part of the house during their tenure in 1820,
before he left England for Italy.
(From a watercolour by Mari Davey 1998)

The Mill-House, Bedhampton, Sussex (*page no.* 96)
Keats and Brown stayed here with the Miller, John Snook in
January 1819. Whilst there Keats wrote the poem 'The Eve
of St Agnes'. He spent his last night in England at the Mill-
House in September 1820 accompanied by Joseph Severn.
(From a watercolour by Mari Davey 2007)

The Keats-Shelley Memorial House and Museum,
Rome, Italy. Piazza di Spagna (The Spanish Steps)
(*page no.* 97)
Where Keats died on 23rd February 1821. Keats and Severn
rented rooms on the second floor during their time together
in Rome, late 1820 to early 1821.
(From a watercolour by Mari Davey 2008)

Keats on his deathbed (*page no.* 98)
From a pen and ink drawing by Joseph Severn 1821.
Severn's caption reads – "28 Jany, 3 o'clock mg. drawn to
keep me awake – A deadly sweat was on him all this
night…" (Keats House, Hampstead.)

IL CIMITERO ACATTOLICO DI ROMA.
The Protestant Cemetery, Rome (*page no.* 99)
The graves of Keats and Severn.

Chronology of the Life and Times of John Keats

1795	Oct. 31	John Keats' birth, Finsbury, London. Exact location unsure.
	Dec. 18	John Keats is christened at St Botolph's Bishopsgate.
1797	Feb. 28	George Keats' birth.
1799	Nov. 18	Thomas Keats' birth.
1801	Apr. 28	Edward Keats' birth (died an infant).
1803	Jun. 03	Frances (Fanny) Mary Keats' birth.
1803–1811		John Keats is educated at John Clarke's School, Enfield.
1804	Apr. 16	Thomas Keats, John's father, is killed in a riding accident.
	Apr. 23	Thomas Keats is buried at St Stephen's, Coleman Street.
	Jun. 27	Keats' mother, Frances, marries William Rawlings at St George's, Hanover Square.
1804–1810		The Keats children live with their grandmother, Alice Jennings, at Edmonton.
1805	Oct. 21	Nelson is killed at the Battle of Trafalgar.
1810	Mar.	Keats' mother, Frances, dies of tuberculosis on 20 Mar. She is buried at St Stephen's.
1811		The madness of King George III – George IV becomes regent. Keats begins his apprenticeship with Dr Thomas Hammond in Edmonton.
1812		Keats writes his poem 'Imitation of Spenser'.
1813		Keats and Joseph Severn become friends.

1814	Dec.	Keats' grandmother, Alice Jennings, dies on 19 Dec. She is buried at St Stephen's.
1815	Feb. 02	Keats writes the sonnet 'Written on the Day that Mr Leigh Hunt Left Prison'.
	Jun. 18	The Battle of Waterloo.
1816	Oct. 01	Keats enters Guy's Hospital as a student.
1816	May. 05	Keats' poem 'O Solitude' is published in the *Examiner*.
	Jul. 25	Keats sits an exam to qualify as an Apothecary.
	Nov.	Keats is introduced to Benjamin Robert Haydon, the classical artist.
	Dec. 01	Keats meets with Leigh Hunt at Hunt's cottage, Vale of Health, Hampstead.
	Dec.	Keats meets Shelley and Horace Smith at Hunt's.
1817	Mar. 03	Keats' first book of poems is published by Olliers.
	Spring	Keats meets Taylor and Hessey (new publishers), also Richard Woodhouse and Benjamin Bailey.
	Apr. 15	At Carisbrooke, Isle of Wight, Keats begins 'Endymion'.
	May. 10	At Margate with his brother Tom, reads over 'Endymion' written so far.
	May. 16	Keats goes alone to Canterbury.
	May. 18	Keats meets Isabella Jones at Bo-Peep, West Hastings.
	Jun. 10	Keats in back in London, lodging at Well Walk, Hampstead.
	Sep. 05	Keats on holiday at Oxford with Benjamin Bailey.
	Oct. 04	Keats visits Stratford-upon-Avon with Bailey.
	Oct. 05	Keats returns from Oxford to Well Walk, Hampstead.

1818	Jun. 25	In the Lake District Keats and Brown call at Dove Cottage, disappointed to find Wordsworth out.
	Jul. 01-31	Keats and Brown on the Scottish walking tour.
	Jul. 11	The travellers visit Robert Burns' cottage and tomb.
	Aug. 07	Keats unwell returns by sea to London alone.
	Aug. 18	Keats arrives at Hampstead.
	Sep.-Dec.	Keats nurses his dying brother Tom at Well Walk.
	Oct.-Nov.	Keats' first meeting with Fanny Brawne.
	Oct.	Keats renews his acquaintance with Isabella Jones. (see Peter Davey's book *A Poet in Love*, 2009).
	Dec. 01	Tom Keats dies; John moves in with Charles Brown at Wentworth Place.
	Dec. 07	Tom Keats' funeral at St Stephen's.
	Dec. 25	Keats spends Christmas Day with the Brawne family; supposed secret engagement to Fanny.
1819	Jan. 21	With Brown at Chichester and Bedhampton, Keats writes 'The Eve of St Agnes'.
	Feb.	Keats returns to Wentworth Place suffering from a sore throat.
	Feb. 13–17	Writes 'The Eve of St Mark' poem unfinished.
	Feb. 22	Keats in town with Taylor. Caught in a snowstorm.
	Feb. 23	Breaks up with Isabella Jones. (see *A Poet in Love*)
	Apr. 11	Keats meets, walks and talks with Samuel Taylor Coleridge in Hampstead.
	Apr.	Keats writes, 'La Belle Sans Merci' – 'Ode to Psyche' and 'Ode on a Grecian Urn'.

1819	May.	Writes 'Ode to a Nightingale'.
	Jun.	Keats very unwell, persistent sore throat.
	Jun. 27	Keats starts out for an escape to the Isle of Wight.
	Jul.	At the Isle of Wight with James Rice and Charles Brown. Keats and Brown begin the play 'Otho the Great' as a joint project.
	Jul. 25	Keats is supposed to have composed the sonnet 'Bright Star'.
	Aug. 12	Keats and Brown journey to Winchester, 'Otho the Great' is finished.
	Aug. 16	The Peterloo Massacre takes place at St Peter's Field, Manchester.
	Sep.	At Winchester, Keats is working on 'Hyperion'.
	Sep. 10–15	Keats leaves Winchester for London on a money-raising quest for his brother George.
	Sep. 15	Keats returns to Winchester. 'Ode to Autumn' is written; 'The Eve of St Agnes' revised.
	Oct.	Begins writing 'The Cap and Bells'.
	Oct. 08	Keats leaves Winchester for London, to live for a short time at 25, College Street, Westminster.
	Oct. 15–16	Keats returns to Hampstead, to lodge with Charles Brown. Fanny Brawne and family next door in Wentworth Place. John becomes a vegetarian.
	Dec.	Keats is unwell, flare up of his sore throat.
1820	Jan.	'Ode on a Grecian Urn' is published in the *Annals of Fine Arts*. The magical spell of poetry-writing comes to an end.
	Feb. 03	Keats taken ill, coughs up blood from his lungs. The beginning of his fatal tuberculosis.

1820	May 04	Keats leaves Wentworth Place for lodgings near to Leigh Hunt in Kentish Town. Brown's part of Wentworth Place is let out for the summer.
	May 07	Brown leaves to begin a holiday in Scotland. Keats accompanies him as far as Gravesend on the Scottish smack. This was to be their final parting, they never met again.
	May 10	'La Belle Dame Sans Merci' is published in *The Indicator*. Death of George III. Disliked by the people, the Prince Regent becomes George IV.
	Jun. 22	Keats' illness worsens at his lodging. Leigh Hunt takes him into his own home and summons a doctor.
	Jun.	Keats' second book of poems is published in the last week of the month.
	Jul. 01	The *Literary Gazette* prints 'Ode to a Nightingale', 'The Mermaid Tavern' and 'Ode to Autumn'.
	Jul. 20	'The Ode to Autumn' appears in *The Literary Chronicle*.
	Jul. 29	'Ode on a Grecian Urn' in *The Literary Chronicle*.
	Aug. 12	Desperately ill Keats returns to Wentworth Place and is nursed by Fanny and her mother.
	Aug.	Reviews of Keats' poems appear in *The New Times*, *The Examiner*, *The Edinburgh Review* and *The Quarterly*. *The Indicator* prints four stanzas of 'The Cap and Bells'.
	Sep. 13	Keats leaves Wentworth Place, Hampstead, to begin his journey to Italy with Joseph Severn.

1820	Sep. 17	Keats boards the *Maria Crowther* in the London Docks and moves down river to Gravesend, several friends accompany him thus far.
	Sep. 18	The *Maria Crowther* sails from Gravesend and encounters a severe storm in the Channel.
	Sep. 20	The ship is becalmed off Dungeness, Keats and Severn go ashore.
	Sep. 28	The *Maria Crowther* puts into Portsmouth for repair. Keats and Severn visit the Snooks at the Mill House Bedhampton. Keats spends his last night in England.
	Sep. 29	The voyage is rejoined, becalmed again. Keats and Severn go ashore to walk at Studland Bay or Lulworth Cove.
	Oct. 21	The *Maria Crowther* arrives at Naples, the ship is put into quarantine.
	Nov. 01	Keats and Severn disembark at Naples.
	Nov. 08	Keats sets out by carriage for Rome.
	Nov. 15	Keats arrives at Rome, Italy.
	Dec. 10	Keats suffers a relapse, from which he does not recover.
1821	Feb. 23	Keats dies at the Piazza di Spagna apartment on the Spanish Steps.
	Feb. 26	Keats' funeral takes place. He is buried in the Protestant Cemetery, Rome, outside the Aurelian Wall.
	Feb.	Napoleon Bonaparte dies on St Helena.
1822		Percy Bysshe Shelley dies, drowned in Italy. Some of his remains are buried near Keats in Rome.

People Named Within This Book

Abbey, Richard – Tea Importer/Merchant. The Keats siblings' guardian.

Angeletti, Anna – Keats and Severn's landlady in Rome.

Brawne, Fanny – Engaged to Keats Dec. 1818.

Brawne, Frances – Fanny's mother.

Brawne, Margaret – (Toots) Fanny's younger sister.

Brawne, Samuel – Fanny's brother.

Brown, Carlino – Charles Brown's son.

Brown, Charles-Armitage – Keats' friend and part owner of Wentworth Place.

Bentley, Mr and Mrs – (Postman) Keats' landlord at Well Walk, Hampstead.

Clarke, Charles Cowden – Keats' teacher at Enfield, close friend.

Clarke, Mary – née Novello. Wife of C.C.C. Writer and friend of Dickens.

Clarke, John – C.C.C.'s father, Headmaster of Clarke's School, Enfield.

Coleridge, Samuel Taylor – Lake poet and philosopher.

Cotterell, Charles – Brother of Miss C. befriends Keats and Severn in Naples, Italy.

Cotterell, Miss – A consumptive passenger on the voyage to Italy.

Dilke, Charles Wentworth – Editor, part owner of Wentworth Place.

Dilke, Charles – Son of C.W.D.

Dilke, Maria – Wife of C.W.D.

Dilke's Mr & Mrs – C.W.D.'s father and mother living at Chichester.

Hammond, Thomas – Doctor, with whom Keats served an apprenticeship.

Haslam, William – Lawyer, friend of the Keats brothers. (Our oak friend)

Haydon, Benjamin Robert – friend of Keats. Historical Painter.

Hessey, James – Keats' publisher, in partnership with John Taylor.

Holmes, Edward – Musician, school fellow of Keats.

Hunt, John – Editor and writer, brother of Leigh.

Hunt, James Henry Leigh – Editor and poet, friend of Keats.

Hunt, Marianne – Wife of Leigh.

Jennings, John and Alice – Keats' grandparents.

Jennings, Lieutenant Midgley – Keats' uncle.

Jones, Isabella – A woman romantically associated with John Keats.

Keats, Frances – The Keats children's mother, née Jennings, later Rawlings.

Keats, Frances (Fanny) – Keats' sister.

Keats, George and Thomas – Keats' brothers.

Keats, John – The poet.

Keats, Thomas – Father to the Keats children.

Lamb, Charles – Critic, writer, and essayist.

Landor, Walter Savage – Poet and writer.

Martin, John – Publisher, friend of Keats and Brown.

Monkton Milnes, Richard – (Lord Houghton) Keats' biographer.

Novello, Vincent – Organist and composer. Father-in-law to C.C.C.

Novello, Sabilla – Vincent's wife.

O'Donaghue, Abigail – Brown's Irish maid servant, mother of his son.

Ollier, C & J – Publishers of Keats' first book of poems.

Reynolds, John Hamilton – Solicitor, writer and poet, friend of Keats.

Rice, James – Lawyer, friend of the Keats brothers, 'often unwell'.

Richard's, Thomas – Clerk of Ordnance at the Tower. School fellow of Keats.

Ryland, Rev: John – Calvinist Minister. Original owner of Clarke's School.

Severn, Joseph – Portrait painter, accompanied Keats to Rome in 1820.

Shelley, Percy Bysshe – Poet, friendly with John Keats.

Shelley, Mary – Husband of P.B.S. née Wollstonecraft – Godwin.

Smith, Horace – Wealthy stockbroker, sponsor of the arts and poet of merit.

Smith, William – Secretary, apprentice to Taylor and Hessey.

Snook, John – Miller at Bedhampton, Dilke's brother-in-law.

Southey, Robert – Poet, philosopher. Poet laureate.

Taylor, John – Keats' publisher, partner James Hessey.

Trelawny, Edward John – Friend of Byron and Charles Armitage-Brown.

Walsh, Thomas – Captain of the brig the *Maria Crowther*.

Woodhouse, Richard – Lawyer, reader for Taylor & Hessey. Friend of Keats.

Wordsworth, William – Lake poet.

Wylie, Georgiana – Wife of George Keats.

The doctors attending Tom and John Keats during their illnesses were:
Dr Bree, Dr Lambe, Dr Rodd, Dr George Darling,
and in Rome Dr James Clark.

Wentworth Place, Hampstead, known as Keats House.

Wentworth Place was built as a joint venture between Charles Armitage-Brown and his friend Charles Wentworth Dilke during the years 1814–16. It was completed by February 1816, but stood empty until the October of that year, when the two friends took up residence. The house was one of the first properties to be built in the Lower Heath Quarter of Hampstead. William Dilke, the younger brother of Charles Wentworth, built his house adjacent to Wentworth Place soon afterwards. Dilke's grandson, the MP Sir Charles Wentworth Dilke, recalled, "It was my great uncle William that painted the name at the gate of Wentworth Place." (Harry Buxton Forman's Keats' biography.) How the cost of the building was shared is unknown, but as Dilke's part of the property was the greater, his portion of the finance is likely to have been larger than Brown's.

Keats House is near the bottom of Keats Grove, formerly John Street. From the front elevation it has the appearance of a detached house, but in Brown and Dilke's time an unbroken wall separated the building into two parts. Keats said that just a wall separated him from Fanny Brawne, today both parts of the house are connected by internal doors.

Steps led to a front door between two large casement windows. This door gave access to the larger, 'eastern', part of the house, which was occupied by Charles and Maria Dilke. Brown, a bachelor, lived in the smaller, western section. His accommodation included front and back sitting rooms on the ground floor, with bedrooms both front and back above them. Keats first began to visit the house in 1817, after he had been introduced to the Dilkes by John Hamilton

Reynolds, the poet solicitor, who was attached to the Leigh Hunt circle of friends.

In December 1818, and after the death of his brother Tom, Brown invited Keats to 'keep house' with him. Brown wrote: "Early one morning I was awakened in my bed by a pressure on my hand. It was Keats, who came to tell me his brother was no more. I said nothing… At length, my thoughts returning from the dead to the living, I said – 'Have nothing more to do with those lodgings – and alone too. Had you not better live with me?' he paused, pressed my hand warmly, and replied, – 'I think it would be better.' From that moment he was my inmate."

Keats paid Brown a rent of £5 a month, and agreed to pay half of the food and liquor bill. Overall Keats lived at the house for fourteen months over a period of almost two years (December 1818 to September 1820), firstly with Brown and later in 1820 when he was nursed during his illness by Fanny Brawne and her mother.

When Keats was with Brown he had use of a sitting room at the back of the house, termed the parlour, his bedroom was also at the back, the windows of both rooms looked out over the smaller garden to the north. When he was taken ill with tuberculosis Brown made up a bed in his sitting room at the front of the house, which gave Keats a view over the roadway and heath.

Both occupants of the property had use of the basement floor, which contained the kitchens, pantries and servants' quarters. It's likely that Abigail O'Donaghue occupied one of the servants' rooms during her employment by Charles Brown. However, in a letter to his brother George in America, Keats mentions hearing Abigail in Brown's bedroom, which was just across the landing from his. He complained about noisy love making!

Brown sold his part of the house to Dilke's father in June 1822 and left England for Italy that same year. The Dilkes had moved out in April 1819, moving to Westminster for their son Charlie's education, letting that part of the house to Mrs Brawne, then a widow, and her three children – Fanny, Margaret (Toots) and Samuel. The Brawnes had briefly rented Brown's part of the property whilst he and Keats were away on their walking tour in the north of England and Scotland in 1818. Fanny Brawne's mother died on the steps of Wentworth Place in December 1829 from burns received after an accident with a candle. By the March of 1830, Fanny with her brother and sister had left the house.

After Keats' death, his sister Francis (Fanny) and Fanny Brawne became friends. Fanny Keats had married Valentin Llanos, a Spanish diplomat and writer. Keats' sister, now Mrs Llanos, lived in what had been Brown's part of the house from 1829 until 1831.

In 1838 Eliza Chester, a retired actress who had been a favourite of George IV, brought the property and converted it into one large house, adding to the western side a large drawing room and conservatory now known as the Chester room. The room is used to house artefacts of Keats and Fanny Brawne, letters and manuscripts etc.

The house was almost continually occupied up until 1920, when it was rescued from demolition by public subscriptions, largely from America. The ownership was transferred to Hampstead Borough Council, now the London Borough of Camden Council which body undertook to maintain the property in perpetuity as a memorial to the poet.

The house was first opened to the public on the 9 May 1925.

During the Second World War it received bomb damage, and was afterwards partially restored by the generosity of the Pilgrim Trust and the Keats-Shelley Association of America Inc, in 1951. In 1974–5, £90,000, a grant by the Historic Buildings Council was spent on a complete restoration, using wallpaper and designs copied from examples of the originals. The house is decorated and furnished in the style of the

1820s. A grant from the National Lottery in 2009 has enabled further improvements.

The Heath Branch Public Library is next to the house, and occupies an area that would once have been the kitchen garden of Wentworth Place. The library was opened to the public on 16 July 1931, and artefacts now in Keats House were originally on display in the front of this building.

It is hoped that the gardens can be restored to their original design and contain flowers and shrubs of the early nineteenth century.

Preface

Keats had many friends, and they are remembered by their association with him, without that association they must surely have passed into obscurity. In a letter to Francis (Fanny) Keats, the poet's sister, dated 18 Sept: 1820, just after Keats had left London for Italy, Fanny Brawne wrote about Keats' devoted friends.

"I am certain he has some spell that attaches them to him, or else he has fortunately met with a set of friends that I did not believe could be found in the world."

The three covered within this book are considered by many to have been his best and most important friends:

Charles Cowden Clarke

Clarke, son of John Clarke, owner and headmaster of 'Clarke's School' at Enfield. Keats' friend during and beyond his schooldays, Charles Cowden Clarke introduced him to poetry. And when Keats began to compose his own poems it was Clarke who recognised the spark of genius. It was Clarke who took the first steps to promote his friend and pupil's work, introducing him to Leigh Hunt. Hunt himself an aspiring poet, immediately recognised something special in the poems before him. Hunt was the first to seriously promote Keats, bringing him to public notice by publishing the poem 'To Solitude' in his weekly newspaper *The Examiner* on the 5th May 1816.

Clarke lived a long, happy and productive life, and fifty years on from the poet's death he still wrote affectionately about Keats, promoting his life and works in the book he wrote in conjunction with his wife Mary, *Recollections of Writers*.

Charles Armitage-Brown

Brown, a businessman, and part owner of Wentworth Place, Hampstead had been drawn into the literary world from the time of his schooldays, when he studied Shakespeare. Long before coming within the Leigh Hunt circle he had written two stories and a play.

He knew of Keats through Hunt, but it was by chance that he first met Keats on the Hampstead Road in 1817. The details of that meeting he claimed remained with him for the rest of his life. At the time Keats' life was in a turmoil, he needed encouragement, and the elder Brown was just the person to give it. Brown invited him home, and thereafter several days a week Keats could be found in Brown's sitting room at Wentworth Place, working on his poetry.

Brown had a steadying effect on the poet, and as for himself he felt that he was in the presence of a superior being. He took it upon himself to preserve Keats' poems, fair copying and cataloguing them. He noticed at that time how careless the poet was with the scraps of paper on which he had scribbled his poems. Brown is owed a debt of gratitude by the literary world for what he did at that time.

In 1818 they went together on the 'Walks in the North' which are well documented. After the death of his brother Tom from tuberculosis in December 1818, Keats was completely alone at the lodgings in Well Walk.

Brown invited him into Wentworth Place, and from then on they were together up until Keats left England for Italy.

After the poet's death, Brown left the country for Italy, taking with him a huge amount of Keats' unpublished material. It was this material, letters and poems that formed the basis of the first Monkton Milnes biography.

In 1835, with his health beginning to fail he returned to England and retirement. He went to live in a small village near Plymouth, where he wrote about and gave lectures on Shakespeare. He gave the very first lecture in England on Keats and his poems at the Plymouth Institute.

All of his later life he devoted to establishing Keats' fame. In 1841 he emigrated with his son Carlino to New Zealand where he died.

Joseph Severn

Severn met Keats in 1813, and they became firm friends. Although Severn was two years senior to Keats, he was junior in mind. It's said that he hero-worshipped the poet, and followed him like a faithful dog. Whether dog-like or no he was certainly faithful, and Keats appreciated him for that.

He is supposed to have said that Severn "Had a gift of giving happiness to others". Severn's friendship with Keats brought him other valuable friends, friends within the Leigh Hunt circle, friends who were able to promote his portrait painting.

He is best remembered for going to Italy with the ailing Keats, and was with him up to the time of his death. Severn became a well-known artist of his day, married well, and lived a good part of a long life in Italy, becoming British Consul at Rome. And retired on a pension from the British Government.

He died in August 1879, and his grave can be found in the old Protestant Cemetery, Rome, next to that of his friend John Keats.

PART I

Charles Cowden Clarke
1787–1877

Charles Cowden Clarke was born on the 15th of December 1787, at Enfield. He was the only son of John Clarke, the owner and headmaster of the school that would become known for the education of John Keats and his brothers George and Tom.

The school was founded by a Calvinist Minister, the Reverend John Ryland, who, before the Enfield school owned another in Northampton where John Clarke had been the headmaster. Clarke married Ryland's stepdaughter. And when his father-in-law moved his school to Enfield, John Clarke and his new wife came with him. The Reverend Ryland wished to retire, and after the first term at the new school he handed the reins to John Clarke.

Clarke's ideas on education did not conform with those of the time. A progressive liberal he based his teaching on humanitarian liberal principles. Students were taught his liberal ideals, ideals unpopular amongst the establishment of the day. In spite of this, like-minded men held on to their integrity. In its own way Clarke's school was part of this. The masters supported their head, and taught the seventy or so boys, whose ages ranged from six to sixteen in the spirit of Clarke's ideas. In the small school at Enfield John Clarke established his own curriculum, differing from the recognised one of the day. *The Hecuba of Euripides* and Thomas Hughes' *Tom Brown's Schooldays* where not the only mental stimulant for boys, as they would in later years become embedded in England's respected but brutal Public Schools. The library shelves at Clarke's school were filled

1

with the classics, history and geography, and prizes were awarded for translations of Latin and French to English. French was taught by Abbé Béliard, a French migrant, who taught Keats to read it, although he did not master the speech. In later years when with Fanny Brawne, who had fluent French, he regretted not having the speech. Clarke had a wide circle of like-minded liberal friends, and senior students were given the chance to meet and talk with these men. In an age when discipline in schools was extremely harsh, instead of punishment Clarke substituted a reward system, awarding prizes to those who did well. He did not try to form his charges into a unit, giving the boys scope to develop individual tastes and characters. This allowed a wide range and variety of interests, producing inventors, artists, writers, lawyers and doctors.

Charles, John Clarke's son, received his education within his father's school, and when he reached the age of fourteen he began to teach the younger boys. When John Keats first came to the school as a child of five or six, the fifteen-year-old Charles Clarke would have given him the greater part of his elementary education and later on helped the young Keats to form his poetic genius. All his life Charles loved the theatre, watching plays when the actresses Mrs Siddons and Miss O'Neill were on stage. His favourite actor was Edmund Kean, who would become the idol of Keats himself. Clarke remembered the young Keats as a difficult child to teach. Although popular amongst the other boys of his age he refused to do anything to please the masters, barely scraping through his lessons. But then at the beginning of January 1809 he returned to school for a new term with a changed attitude that surprised both his friends and the teachers.

He determined, as Charles Cowden Clarke recalled, "To carry off all the prizes for literature." This change seems to have coincided with his mother's return to the family. He had now to make up for his past inattention and education lost.

Like at other times throughout his life he went to the extreme. A huge effort would be required for success and he gave it his all. He was the first to get up in the mornings to get at the books. He read in the morning, afternoon and evening. And if he were sent out from the classroom he could be found walking with a book up to his face. At meal times he had a book by his plate. In a short time he had worked his way through every book in the library. The object of these endeavours, to win the school's top prize. During this intense period of self-education he stuffed his mind with a vast amount of information. Information that would prove invaluable as he trod the path to immortality. By the end of the 1809 midsummer term he had reached his objective, winning the literary first prize which was C.H.Kauffman's *Dictionary of Merchandise for the use of Counting Houses*, the headmaster's choice in a school that catered for the sons of the trading and merchant classes. But likely not the ideal book for the boy of a poetical literary bent. At Clarke's school the spirit in John Keats was given space to grow, but it was Charles, the headmaster's son, who would have the greatest influence on the young Keats. From early on the younger Clarke recognised the boy's spark of genius and decided to make himself responsible for any extra education Keats needed. Charles Clarke was for his age very well read. He loved the classics and poetry, and studied contemporary writers such as Coleridge, Lamb, Leigh Hunt and Hazlitt.

The school at Enfield was about ten miles from the centre of London, surrounded by meadows and fields, intermingled with beautiful hedge-lined lanes. It stood near a bend in the New River, where in the summer the boys swam. Through the nearby trees on a wooded slope the remains of Enfield Chase could be seen from the upper school windows. Past the Chase, further on, the road finished at Ponders End where the Keats siblings' grandparents lived before their grandmother Alice moved to Edmonton after the death of her husband John Jennings. The school was a substantial property built by a West India merchant. Above the door, the

3

date, 1717. The house was said to be the birthplace of Isaac Disraeli in 1766. In 1849 it was purchased by the Eastern Counties Railway, becoming a station on the line that ran from Cambridge to Ware and Enfield. In 1872 the building was demolished and a new station built on the site. A large part of the front elevation preserved was restored and erected in the Victoria and Albert museum. The workmanship of the restoration was superb, the rich coloured small red bricks faced up to make for a perfect fit being joined together with beeswax and resin.

In his old age Charles Cowden Clarke described what he remembered of the school when he wrote: "The house was airy, roomy and substantial; especially fitted for a school; the eight bedded room, the six bedded room, as they were called, gives some idea of the dimensions of the apartments. The schoolroom which occupied the site, where formerly had been the coach house and stabling, was forty feet long; the playground was a spacious courtyard between the schoolroom and the house. In this playground there flourished a goodly baking pear tree; and it was made a point of honour with the boys, that if they forbore from touching the fruit until fit for gathering, they would have it in due time for supper regales, properly baked or stewed. From the playground stretched a garden of one hundred yards in length, where in one corner were some small plots set aside for certain boys fond of having a garden of their own. Further on was a sweep of greensward, beyond which existed a pond; sometimes dignified as 'The Lake'. Round this pond sloped strawberry beds, the privilege of watering which was awarded to 'Assiduous boys' on summer evenings, with the due understanding that they would have their share of the juicy red berries when fully ripe. At the far end of the pond, beneath the iron railings which divided our premises from the meadow, beyond whence the song of the nightingales would reach us in the stillness of a May night; there stood a rustic arbour, where John Keats and I used to sit and read Spenser's 'Faery Queene' together. When he had left school,

4

and used to come over from Edmonton, where he was apprenticed to Thomas Hammond the surgeon. On the other side of the house lay a small enclosure which we called 'the drying ground' and where was a magnificent morello cherry tree. Beyond this, a gate led into a small field or paddock of two acres, this the pasture ground for two cows that supplied the establishment with fresh and abundant milk. Not far from the house in some high trees there was a rookery. The boys would watch the birds coming home to roost in the evenings".

Clarke was an old man when he wrote this. He tried to remember Keats as a small boy who came to the school still wearing the child's 'frock', however the distance of the years blurred his memory, he was unable to recall the young Keats' features. He remembered that his own mother became attached to the likeable little boy. He recalled the Keats boy's parents visiting the school; they arrived in a smart gig driven by their father Thomas Keats. He said that his own father John Clarke thought that Keats' parents had 'Fine common sense and respectability'. The visits by Thomas Keats were destined not to last long for in 1804 he was killed in a fall from his horse. "As a small boy Keats had no outward signs of genius about him. As he grew, just like any other boy he enjoyed playing rather than working at his lessons. He had abundant courage and loved to fight and would fight with any other boy at any time. When his youngest brother Tom joined George and himself at school all three were proud of their uncle, Lieutenant Midgley Jennings. The story of his valour at the battle of Camperdown, where it was said he moved about the deck of his ship to detract fire from his captain had spread amongst the schoolboys. Maybe John thought that he had a family reputation to live up to. This was left to him alone, for George the biggest and strongest of the brothers was a placid fellow who spent a good deal of time getting John out of scrapes."

Edward Holmes, one of Keats' schoolfellows and a close friend at the time, said of him: "He was a boy whom anyone from his extraordinary vivacity and personal beauty might easily fancy would become great. But rather in some military capacity than literature. In all the active exercises he excelled, his mood would always be in the extreme, either in a passion of tears or fits of outrageous laughter. His qualities captivated other boys, and he was very popular, although he made few close friends, his brothers were so dear to him that probably they were all he needed."

Maybe, just maybe, Keats' violent behaviour was in some measure an outlet for the creative power already struggling within him. In *his Recollections of Writers* C.C.C. writing about Keats' time at school recalled, "Here it was that John Keats all but commenced and did complete his education. He was born on the 29th of October 1795 and was one of the little fellows who had not wholly emerged from the child's costume (smock-like dress) upon being placed under my father's care. I remember that he had a brisk winning face and was a favourite with all, particularly my mother. John was the only one of the Keats boys resembling his father in person and feature, with brown hair and dark hazel eyes. His brothers George and Thomas, younger than himself, were like their mother, who was tall, of good figure, with a large oval face. Fanny, their sister, much younger, I remember seeing her once walking in the garden with her brothers. My mother spoke of her with fondness for her pretty and simple manners. She married Mr Llanos, a Spanish refugee, a man of liberal principles, very attractive bearing and more than ordinary accomplishments."

C.C.C. continues, "In the early part of his school life, John gave no extraordinary indications of intellectual character, but there was ever present a determined and steady spirit in all his undertakings, I never knew it misdirected in his required pursuit of study. The future ramifications of that noble genius were then closely shut in seed, his passion at times was almost ungovernable. His brother George being considerably taller and stronger, used to hold him down by main force, laughing when John was in one of his moods and was endeavouring to beat him. It was however a wisp-of-straw conflagration for he had an intensely tender affection for his brothers and proved it upon the most trying occasions.

"I never heard a word of disapproval from anyone superior or equal who had known him. Leigh Hunt's *Examiner* which my father took in, I used to lend to Keats and this no doubt laid the foundation of his love of civil and religious liberty. He left our school aged fourteen and was apprenticed to Thomas Hammond a medical man, residing in Church Street, Edmonton, two miles from Enfield; this arrangement evidently gave him satisfaction, and I fear that this was the most placid period of his painful life, for now with the exception of the duty he had to perform in the surgery, by no means an onerous one, his whole leisure hours were employed in indulging his passion for reading and translating. During his apprenticeship he finished the *Aeneid*.

"The distance between our residences being so short, I gladly encouraged his inclination to come over when he could claim a leisure hour. And in consequence I saw him about five or six times a month on my own leisure afternoons. When the weather permitted, we always sat in an arbour at the end of the spacious garden.

"It is difficult at this lapse of time, to note the spark that fired the train of his poetical tendencies." (Charles Cowden Clarke wrote his recollections of John Keats in 1858, some thirty-seven years after Keats' death.) C.C.C. continues – "At that time he may have been sixteen years old, when I read to him the 'Epithalamion of Spenser' he certainly appreciated the general beauty of the composition and felt the more passionate passages, for his features and exclamations were ecstatic. How often in after times have I heard him quote these lines:

Behold, while she before the altar stands,
Hearing the holy priest that to her speaks,
And blesses her with his two happy hands
How the red roses flush up her cheeks!

"That night he took away with him the first volume of Spenser's *Faerie Queene* and he went through it as I formerly told his noble biographer. 'As a young horse would through a spring meadow – ramping!' Like a true poet, to a poet born, not manufactured, a poet in grain, he especially singled out epithets, for that felicity and power in which Spenser is so eminent. He hoisted himself up, looked burly and dominant, as he said, 'what an image that is' – 'sea shouldering whales'! It was a treat to see as well as hear him read a pathetic passage. Once, when reading the *Cymbeline* aloud, I saw his eyes fill with tears and his voice faltered when he came to the departure of Posthumus from Imogen; saying she would have watched him –

'Till the diminution
Of space had pointed him sharp as my needle;
Nay follow'd him till he had melted from
The smallest of a gnat to air; and then
Have turn'd mine eye and wept.

"I cannot remember the precise time of our separating at this stage of Keats' career, or which of us first went to London; but it was upon an occasion when walking together to see Leigh Hunt, who had just fulfilled his penalty of confinement in Horsemonger Lane Prison for the unwise libel upon the Prince Regent, that Keats met me and turning, accompanied me back part of the way. At the last field gate, when taking leave, he gave me the sonnet entitled 'Written on the day that Mr Leigh Hunt left Prison'. This the first proof of his having committed himself in verse. I recall the conscious look and hesitation with which he offered it! Biographers have stated that 'The Lines in Imitation of Spenser' are the earliest known verses of his composition, the subject being the inspiration of his first love of poetry, and such a love."

Now morning from her orient chamber came,
And her first footsteps touch'd a verdant hill –

However Keats' first published poem was the sonnet 'O Solitude'.

C.C.C. continued, "When we both came to London, Keats to enter as a student at Guy's hospital" (Clarke mistakenly wrote St Thomas's hospital) "he was not long in discovering my abode, which was with a brother-in-law in Clerkenwell, and at the time being housekeeper and solitary, he would come and renew his loved gossip, till, as the author of the 'Urn Burial' says, 'we were acting our antipodes'. The huntsmen were up in America, and they already past their first sleep in Persia.'

"At the close of a letter which preceded my appointing him to come and lighten my darkness in Clerkenwell, in his first address upon coming to London he says, 'although the Borough is a beastly place in dirt, turnings, and windings, yet No: 8 Dean Street, is not difficult to find.'

To Charles Cowden Clarke.
Wednesday 11 Oct. 1815.

[There was no address or postmark.]

My dear Sir,

The busy time has just gone by, and I can now devote any time you may mention to the pleasure of seeing Mr Hunt t'will be an Era in my existence – I am anxious to see the Author of the Sonnet to the Sun, for it is no mean gratification to become acquainted with men who in their admiration of Poetry do not jumble together Shakespeare and Darwin – I have copied out a sheet or two of verses which I composed some time ago, and find so much to blame in them that the worst part will go into the fire – those to G. Matthew I will suffer to meet the eye of Mr H. not withstanding that the Muse is so frequently mentioned. I here sinned in the face of Heaven even while remembering what, I think, Horace says, "never presume to make a God appear but for an Action worthy of a God" (Ars Poetica 191). [Keats omitted the final quotes, he had probably read the Earl of Roscommon's version: 'Never presume to make a God appear, But for a Business worthy of a God.'] From a few words of yours when last I saw you, I have no doubt but that you have something in your Portfolio which I should by rights see – I will put you in Mind of it. Although the Borough is a beastly place in dirt, turnings and windings; yet No: 8 Dean Street is not difficult to find. And if you would run the Gauntlet over London Bridge take the first turning to the left and then the first to the right and moreover knock at my door which is nearly opposite a Meeting, you would do one a Charity which as St Paul saith is the father of all the Virtues – At all events let me hear from you soon – I say at all events not excepting the Gout in your fingers.

Yours sincerely
John Keats

"This letter preceded our first symposium, and a memorable night it was in my life's career. We were in possession of the Homer of Chapman and to work we went, turning to some of the 'famousest' passages, as we had scrappily known them in Pope's version. There was for instance that perfect scene of the conversion on Troy wall of the old Senators with Helen, who is pointing out to them the several Greek Captains. One scene I could not fail to introduce to him was the shipwreck of Ulysses in the fifth book of *The Odyssey*. And I had the reward of one of his delighted stares upon reading the following lines" –

Then forth he came, his both knees falt'ring, both
His strong hands hanging down, and all with froth
His cheeks and nostrils flowing, voice and breath
Spent to all use, and down he sank to death.

The sea had soak'd his heart through; all his veins
His toils had rack'd t'a labouring woman's pains.
Dead – weary was he.

"It was proof of his wonderment, that when I came down to breakfast the next morning, I found upon my table a letter with no other enclosure than his famous sonnet"–

~ *On First Looking into Chapman's Homer* ~

Much have I travell'd in the realms of gold
And many goodly states and kingdoms seen;
Round many western islands have I been
Which bards in fealty to Apollo hold.
Oft of one wide expanse had I been told
That deep-brow'd Homer ruled as his demesne;
Yet did I never breathe its pure serene
Till I heard Chapman speak out loud and bold:
Then felt I like some watcher of the skies
When a new planet swims into his ken;
Or like stout Cortez when with eagle eyes
He star'd at the Pacific – and all his men
Look'd at each other with a wild surmise –
Silent, upon a peak in Darien.

(October 1816)

"We had parted, as I have already said, at days spring, [day break] yet he contrived that I should receive the poem from a distance of, maybe two miles by ten o'clock."

When the sonnet was published the seventh line was altered – in the original which he sent to Clarke it read:

'Yet could I never tell what men could mean.'

This he said was bold, and too simply wondering.

His favourite among Chapman's 'Hymns of Homer' was the one to Pan, which he rivalled in Endymion with these lines:

O'thou whose mighty palace roof doth hang,
From jagged trunks, and overshadoweth

11

Eternal whispers, glooms, the birth, life, death
Of unseen flowers in heavy peacefulness;
Who lov'st to see the hamadryads dress
Their ruffled locks where meeting hazels darken;
And through whole solemn hours dost sit, and harken
The dreary melody of bedded reeds –
In desolate places, where dank moisture breeds
The pipy hemlock to strange overgrowth;
Bethinking thee, how melancholy loth
Thou wast to lose fair Syrinx – do thou now,
By thy love's milky brow!
By all the trembling mazes that she ran,
Hear us, great Pan!

This stanza appears in book one of the long poem 'Endymion'; the first line of which is recognised by all as a proverb:

"A thing of beauty is a joy for ever"

C.C.C. wrote: "In one of our conversations about this period, I alluded to his position at Guy's Hospital. I had taken for granted that the profession had been his own selection, and not chosen for him. He at once made no secret of his inability to sympathise with the science of anatomy, as a main pursuit in life. One of the expressions he used in describing his unfitness for its mastery was perfectly characteristic. 'The other day for instance, during the lecture, there came a sunbeam into the room, and with it a whole troop of creatures floating in the ray; and I was off with them to Oberon and fairyland.' I was afterwards informed that at his subsequent examination he displayed an amount of acquirement which surprised his fellow students (the Apothecary examination). He once talked with me upon my complaining of stomachic derangement, with a remarkable decision of opinion, describing the functions and actions of the organ with the clearness, and I presume, technical precision of an adult practitioner; casually illustrating the comment in his characteristic way, with poetical imagery:

'the stomach,' he said, 'being like a brood of callow nestlings (opening his capacious mouth!) yearning and gaping for sustenance.' And indeed he merely exemplified what should be if possible, the stock in trade of every poet: viz, to know all that there is to be known 'in the heaven above, or in the earth beneath, or in the waters under the earth'."

C.C.C. wrote about the time that he took some of Keats' poems to show Leigh Hunt. Clarke was surprised by the reception the poems received having introduced them as the work of a young man still a teenager. Hunt began to read 'How Many Bards' and after a few lines expressed his admiration. Horace Smith a wealthy stockbroker, sponsor of the arts and a poet of merit who happened to be at the Vale of Health Cottage, read with approval the last but one line. 'That distance of recognizance bereaves'. "What a well-condensed expression for a youth so young!" Smith had immediately recognised the spark of genius. Leigh Hunt requested Clarke to bring Keats with him on his next visit.

C.C.C. wrote: "About this time Keats left the neighbourhood of the Borough, and took up lodgings together with his brothers in apartments on the second floor of a house in the Poultry, over the passage leading to the Queens Head Tavern and opposite to one of the City Companies halls. The Ironmongers if I mistake not. I have the associating reminiscence of many happy hours spent in this abode. Here was determined upon, in great part written, and sent forth to the world, the first little but vigorous offspring of his brain. Poems by John Keats. 'What more felicity can fall to a creature'. *[Fate of the Butterfly; Spenser]*

"The book was printed in London by C & J Ollier of Welbeck Street, Cavendish Square. And here on the evening when the last proof sheet was brought from the printer, there came a request from the publishers for a dedication." C.C.C. remembered his part in the dedication: "The poem which commences the volume, says Lord Houghton in his first memoir of the poet; was suggested to Keats by a delightful summer's day. As he stood beside the gate that leads from the battery on Hampstead Heath into a field by Caen Wood." C.C.C.– "The following lovely passage he himself told me was the recollection of our having frequently loitered over the rail of a footbridge that spanned a little brook in the last field upon entering Edmonton."

> Linger awhile upon some bending planks
> That lean against a streamlet's rushy banks.

The two-line quotation comes from the poem. 'I Stood tiptoe Upon a Little Hill' and the sixth stanza. This stanza is very long and we continue with the next six lines.

> And watch intently Nature's gentle doings:
> They will be found softer than ring-dove's cooings.
> How silent comes the water round that bend;
> Not the minutest whisper does it send
> To the o'erhanging sallows: blades of grass
> Slowly across the chequer'd shadows pass.

C.C.C. – "I remember the occasion that Keats was first introduced to Chaucer. One day he found me asleep on his sofa, with a volume of Chaucer open at the 'Flower and Leaf'. He expressed his admiration of the poem and gave me his opinion of it, afterwards pointing out a sonnet that he had written on the blank space leaf at the end of the volume. The title was very long, for he had entitled it. 'Written on the blank space of a leaf at the end of Chaucer's – Tale of the Floure and the Lefe'. It was an extempore effusion without a word altered or crossed out. I have it before me now, signed J.K Feb: 1817."

> This pleasant tale is like a little copse:
> The honied lines do freshly interlace
> To keep the reader in so sweet a place,
> So that he here and there full-hearted stops;
> And oftentimes he feels the dewy drops
> Come cool and suddenly against his face,

And by the wandering melody may trace
Which way the tender-legged linnet hops.
Oh! what a power hath white simplicity!
What mighty power has this gentle story!
I that for ever feel a thirst for glory,
Could at this moment be content to lie
Meekly upon the grass, as those whose sobbings
Were heard of none beside the mournful robins.

(February 27th, 1817)

"This occasion was I believe, Keats' first introduction to Chaucer's *Troilus and Cresseide*' These two circumstances associated with my friend's literary career have stamped a priceless value upon my own miniature 18-mo copy of Chaucer.

"When the first volume of Keats' minor muse was launched. Everyone of us amid his circle expected that it would create a sensation in the literary world, for such a first production had rarely occurred. The three Epistles, and seventeen sonnets, including 'On First Looking into Chapmans Homer' would have ensured a rousing welcome from our modern day reviewers. [C.C.C. is writing almost fifty years after the event.] Alas! The book might have emerged in 'Timbuktu' with far stronger chance of fame and approbation. It never passed to a second edition; the first was small, and never sold off. The word had been passed that its author was Radical; and in those days of 'Bible, Crown and Constitution' he might have had more success had he been Anti-Jacobin."

Keats had not made any demonstrations of his political opinion, but to show gratitude for his encouragement, he had dedicated his book to Leigh Hunt, the editor of *The Examiner*, a recognised radical accused of being a supporter of the so-called Corsican Monster 'Napoleon'. Such an association was enough to damage the work of the young poet. C.C.C. writes. "Can men now utter a word in favour of civil liberty without being chalked on the back and hounded out!" Poor Keats, little did he anticipate the treatment that was waiting for him upon the publication of his next book; 'Endymion'. The work was ridiculed, and the attacks against him were almost vitriolic.

In the space between the two publications he moved from the Poultry to take fresh lodgings in Well Walk, Hampstead, at the home of Mr Bentley the postman. The house was the first or second property on the right-hand side going up to the Heath. C.C.C. wrote: "He came to me one Sunday and we passed most of the day walking, his constant friend Severn was present and Keats read to us portions of 'Endymion' of which he himself was pleased. And never will I forget his expression as he quoted the now celebrated 'Hymn of Pan' from the first book".

Keats could thank for his introduction to Joseph Severn an old school fellow, Edward Holmes, who had been a child scholar at Enfield. He was one that came there like Keats, wearing the child's frock-dress of the time. C.C.C. wrote: "Holmes ought to have been given music lessons from his childhood, for the passion was in him. I used to amuse myself with the pianoforte after supper when all had gone to bed. Upon some occasion leaving the parlour, I heard a scuffle on the stairs, and discovered that my young gentleman had left his bed to hear the music. At length he entrusted to me his heart's secret, that he should like to learn music. When I taught him his tonic alphabet, he soon knew and could do as much as his tutor. Upon leaving school, which he did, I think before he was of age, he was apprenticed to the elder Seely the bookseller. He did not lose sight of his old master, and I introduced him to Mr Vincent Novello, the celebrated musician, organist and composer a friend of mine who not only gave Holmes instruction but took him into his house and made him one of the family, and he resided with them for some years. I was also fortunate in recommending him to the proprietor of the *Atlas* newspaper. And to that journal over a long period he contributed essays and critiques on the science and practice of music, which raised the journal into a reference and authority in the art. He wrote for the *Atlas* a little book of criticism 'A Ramble among the Musicians in Germany'. Later, as a contributor to the *Musical Times*, he produced a series of masterly essays on the music of Haydn, Mozart and Beethoven. His favourite production was the 'Life of Mozart', contriving by means of the great musician's letters to produce an autobiography."

C.C.C. wrote. "In after years, when Keats was reading to me the part of the poem 'The Eve of St Agnes' where Porphyro is listening to the midnight music coming from the hall below.

The kettle drum and far heard clarinet,
Affray his ears, though but in dying tone
The hall door shuts again, and all the noise is gone.

"That line, he said, came into my head when I remembered how I used to listen in bed to your music at school. How enchanting would be a record of the 'gems' and first causes of all great artists conceptions! The elder Brunel's first hint for his shield in constructing the tunnel under the Thames was taken from watching the labour of a sea insect, which, having a projecting hood, could bore into the ships' timbers unmolested by the waves. It may have been about this time that Keats gave an example of his courage and stamina, in the recorded instance of his pugilistic contest with a butcher's boy. He told me in his characteristic manner, of their 'passage of arms'. The brute, he said, was tormenting a kitten, and he interfered. When a threat offered was enough for his mettle, and they 'set to', he thought he should be beaten, for the fellow was the taller and stronger. But like an authentic pugilist, my young poet found that he had planted a blow which told upon his antagonist. In every succeeding round, therefore (for they fought nearly an hour) he never failed of returning to the weak point, and the contest ended in the hulk being led home."

C.C.C. also wrote, "In my knowledge of fellow beings, I never knew one who so thoroughly combined the sweetness with the power of gentleness, and the irresistible sway of anger, as Keats. His indignation would have made the boldest grave. And they who had seen him under the influence of injustice and meanness of soul would not forget the expression of his features. The form of his visage was changed. Upon one occasion, when some local tyranny was being discussed, he amused the party by shouting; 'Why is there not a human dust hole, into which to tumble such fellows?'" C.C.C. quotes out of context here. The quote comes from Benjamin Haydon's journal. Keats had been asked by Leigh Hunt to tidy the Vale of Health Cottage after Hunt had left for Marlow with Shelley to escape his creditors who were hard pressing for payment. Keats had swept dust and rubbish into a dust hole under the floorboards. Afterwards, discussing the episode with Haydon he said 'what a pity there is not a human dust hole!' Haydon deduced that this remark was being applied to Hunt.

C.C.C. wrote. "Keats had a strong sense of humour, (in fact he loved the grotesque). His perception of humour and the power of transmitting it by imitation was both vivid and amusing. He once described to me a bear-baiting, the animal the property of a Mr Tom Oliver. The performance had not begun, and Keats near to, watched a young aspirant, who had brought a younger boy under his wing to witness the solemnity, and whom he oppressively patronised. Now and then in his zeal to manifest and impart his knowledge he would forget himself, and stray beyond the prescribed bounds into the ring, to the lashing resentment of its comptroller Mr William Soames, who after some hints of a practical nature to 'keep back' began laying about him with indiscriminate and unmitigable vivacity. The peripatetic signifying to his pupil 'My eyes! Bill Soames giv me sich a licker'! Evidently grateful, and considering himself complimented upon being included in the general dispensation. Keats' entertainment and appreciation of this minor scene of low life has often recurred to me. But his concurrent personification of the baiting, with his position – his legs and arms bent and shortened till he looked like Bruin on his hind legs, dabbing his fore paws hither and thither as the dogs snapped at him. And now and then acting the gasp of one that had been suddenly caught and hugged. His own capacious mouth adding force to the personation was a remarkable and memorable display. I am ever reminded of this amusing relation by the picture in Shakespeare's *Henry VI* " –

As a bear encompass'd round with dogs,
Who having pinch'd a few and made them cry'
The rest stand all aloof and bark at him.

C.C.C. continued: "Keats also attended a prize fight between the most skilful Light Weights of the day, Randal and Turner; and in describing the rapidity of the blows of the one, while the other was falling, he tapped his fingers on the window pane."

Charles Cowden Clarke wrote: "We record these events in his life because they are characteristic of a natural man. But the partaking in such exhibitions did not for one moment blunt the gentler emotions of his heart, or vulgarise his inborn love of all that was beautiful and true. Had he been born in squalor, he would have emerged a gentle man.

"From Well-Walk he moved to Wentworth Place to cohabit with another firm friend, Charles Armitage Brown. Keats never had a more zealous, a firmer, or more practical friend and adviser than Brown. They accompanied each other on a Scottish Tour, a worthy event in the poet's career. Leading as it did to some fine poems and letters, including the sonnet to 'Ailsa-Rock'. As a passing observation, and to show how the minutest circumstance did not escape him, he told me that when he first came upon the view of Loch-Lomond the sun was setting, the lake was in shade, and of a deep blue. And at the further end was 'a slash across it of deep orange'." The

19

description of the traceried window in the 'Eve of St Agnes' is proof of Keats' intense feeling for colour.

It was early in his time at Wentworth Place that the savage attacks on his person and on his long poem 'Endymion' appeared in some magazines and papers of the day. These articles were directed at what they termed the 'Cockney School' of poetry. Leigh Hunt was elected principal and those writers connected to him in any way were tarred with the same broad brush. To say that these attacks did not affect the consciousness and sensitive self-respect of Keats would be false. He did resent the insults, and they no doubt injured him. But if his tormentors, or Lord Byron, even for a moment supposed that he was crushed, or cowed in spirit by the treatment he had received, never were they more mistaken; 'Snuffed out by an article' indeed! Hazlitt became drawn into the dispute, when an attack was launched against his person. (Hazlitt had a letter published in which he attacks his attackers) "To pay those fellows in their own coin, the way would be to begin with Walter Scott, and have at his clump foot!" Lord Houghton (Monkton Milnes) in his life of Keats, will be full authority for my estimate of Lord Byron, 'Johnny Keats had indeed a small body with a mighty heart' and showed it in the best way; by not fighting the 'Bush Wackers' in their own style, though he could have done so. He resolved to produce brain work which not one of their party could match, and he did so, for in the months from the spring of 1819 into 1820 he produced his very best work; 'The Eve of St Agnes', 'La-Belle Dame sans Merci', the famous odes 'On a Grecian Urn', 'To a Nightingale' and many more. (This was the period Gittings termed 'The Living Year'.) All this wonderful work produced in a period of scarcely more than a year, to prove what his brain could achieve in health.

But alas the disease which would destroy him approached. Upon the publication of his last volume of poems, Charles Lamb wrote one of his fine appreciative critiques in the

Morning Chronicle. C.C.C. wrote: "At that period I had been absent for some weeks from London, and had not heard of the dangerous state of Keats' health, only that he and Severn were going to Italy. It was therefore an unprepared shock which brought me the news of his death in Rome." Charles Cowden Clarke's 'Recollections of Keats' first appeared in a magazine *The Atlantic Monthly* in January 1861 when Clarke was already aged seventy. He recalled the atmosphere of the time in which the poet lived if not exactly the facts of his life, for he was endeavouring to recall events that had taken place many years before.

In their joint publication, the book *Recollections of Writers* Charles and Mary Clarke remembered all of the poets and writers that they had known during their long lives, including Charles Dickens a close friend of Mary. This work grew from the very first recollection, which was by C.C.C. of John Keats. "Our friends were so pleased and interested in the school fellow's recollection," wrote Mary Cowden Clarke, "that they asked for other recollections of writers known to both husband and wife." The *Recollections of Keats*, with a few updates appeared again in the *Gentleman's Magazine* for February 1874. And from August 1875 to July 1876 this magazine serialised the essays of other famous literary men known to the Clarkes. In 1877 Charles Cowden Clarke died, and after her husband's death Mary brought all of the essays together, and they were published in book form. In this venture she had the assistance of Mary Lamb, who added an essay of her own, on her brother Charles Lamb. Mary Lamb's essay had also previously appeared in the *Gentleman's Magazine* of 1873. The Cowden Clarkes were very close friends of Leigh Hunt, and the chapter on Leigh Hunt is the longest in their book. Details on the lives of the Cowden Clarkes are included there. The marriage of Charles and Mary, and parts of the Clarkes' lives after Keats can also be found within the Charles Lamb story. In these recollections the drinking habits of both Keats and Lamb have been glossed over. Although both poet and essayist enjoyed wine, the essayist to a greater degree than the poet.

B.R. Haydon in his journal, overstated the drinking habits of Keats, saying that once for a period of six weeks he never saw Keats but he was under the influence of alcohol, and to this he added his infamous 'Cayenne Pepper' story. Others of the poet's friends, leaping to his defence, have gone in the opposite direction. However, Keats never denied that he enjoyed wine. He celebrated claret in his verse, and wrote about it in his letters, but he was not a drunkard.

The Clarkes were noted for looking on the bright side of life. Nothing really unpleasant seemed to happen to them or their friends, and to this end they wrote nothing derogatory about anyone. Admirable indeed, but sometimes true characters become obscured. The fact that both Charles and Mary had for parents liberal-minded and intelligent people, John Clarke the schoolmaster, and Vincent Novello, the half Italian musician, organist and composer, produced offspring of similar character. John Clarke's wife, the stepdaughter of his old employer the Reverend John Ryland, met when Clarke was teaching within Ryland's school in Northampton. Another young teacher at the school was George Dyer, a scholar in Greek. Both Clarke and Dyer were interested in courting Miss Ann Isabella Scott. Dyer cherished his love secretly, whilst Charles openly declared his and was accepted. Mary Victoria Novello's mother, Mary Sabilla Novello, was half German, a singer and musician, with a famous opera singer sister Clara. Sabilla Novello confirmed the opinion that intellectual and cultivated women are frequently gentle, and proficient housewives. Both John Clarke and Vincent Novello, with their intelligent wives, socialised amongst clever people, and cultivated these relations for their children. With this background of interest and activities they became deeply involved within the Leigh Hunt, Charles Lamb circles. There was hardly anyone in the world of literature, music and theatre at the time with whom they were not in some way connected.

When Charles Cowden Clarke first met Vincent Novello's daughter Mary in 1816, she was but a child of maybe five or six years old, and she was barely seventeen when they married in 1828, she being twenty years his junior. The marriage, in spite of the age difference, was a happy but childless one. Their shared interests of music and literature formed and gave them a common ground. When the Reverend Ryland left Northampton with his family to settle in Enfield, at the time considered to be one of the loveliest villages in England, John and Ann Clarke came with him. Soon the school was formed in a house exactly right for a school. Charles Cowden Clarke became friendly with Vincent Novello, who he only knew by sight. When at a young age he asked Novello to write some sheet music for him; as Clarke said. "I requested music the more legible for my limited knowledge. Novello suggested that I collect the rewritten score from his home at 240 Oxford Street." After this, Clarke said, "And then began the happiest period of my existence."

The Novellos gave musical evenings at home, where the guests might be Leigh Hunt, Shelley, Keats, Charles Lamb and others. Musical supper parties took place at the homes of the Novellos the Hunts and the Lambs. At these gatherings it was agreed the fare would be bread and cheese, with celery, and Lutheran beer. The group organised visits to the theatre, and in the summer they went on picnics in the fields between the west end of Oxford Street and the western slope of Hampstead Hill. "It was on a bright afternoon in the early days of my visits to Leigh Hunt at the Vale of Health", (Little Mary Novello wrote) that she first had sight of her husband-to-be (Charles Cowden Clarke). "When we first saw each other, had some prescient whispered in the ear of each in turn, 'you see your future wife, and that is your husband'," the prediction would have seemed strange. While she was a little girl, there with her parents for a day on the Heath with the Hunt children, thinking, Charles Clarke as she heard him called was a good-natured gentleman. "It would be ten more years after this meeting that we began to think of each other with any deeper feelings."

When Charles Clarke's father John retired from the Enfield School the family moved to Ramsgate, a favourite place with the family, for it was there that they had enjoyed summer holidays. Charles lived there with his parents for a time. Certainly up until his father's death in December 1820.

Whilst at Ramsgate he was approached by Leigh Hunt, wanting verse contributions for his new *Literary Pocket Book*. This pocket book was first published in 1819 smartly bound in Red-Morocco leather.

Clarke wrote. "I was among those to whom he applied, and it was with no small elation that I found myself for the first time in print under the wing of Leigh Hunt."

Hunt produced his pocket book over four years 1819/22.

The second publication included Charles Cowden Clarke's 'Walks round London' in which he described his favourite haunts to the south-west of Enfield. He also contributed some verse, entitled 'On Visiting a Beautiful Little Dell near Margate'. Charles Clarke felt himself in hallowed company amongst the other contributors, Shelley, Keats, Proctor (Barry Cornwall), Charles Ollier and Leigh Hunt himself. Keats rather mocked the book, saying 'it was full of the most sickening stuff'!

In 1821 Leigh Hunt brought a passage to Italy, taking with him his large family. He would join up with Shelley in a new venture. Beaten about with storms in the channel, as had Keats and Severn aboard the *Maria Crowther* eighteen months before, the 120-ton *Jane* was forced to make a landfall at Ramsgate for minor repairs. The Clarkes were surprised when the bedraggled Hunt tribe arrived at the door of their Ramsgate house, where Keats' old schoolmaster had so recently passed away.

Charles Cowden Clarke had been away from London for three years and contact with his poet friend John Keats had been lost. It was Leigh Hunt who broke the news of the serious state of Keats' health and that under the doctor's advice he had, in company with Joseph Severn, taken ship to Italy. Keats and Clarke were never to meet again for the poet died in the February of 1821, just a few weeks after John Clarke his old schoolmaster.

That same year, walking on the East Cliff at Ramsgate, C.C.C. saw Samuel Taylor Coleridge. Clarke said, "He was contemplating the sea under its most attractive aspect: in a dazzling sun, with sailing clouds that drew their purple shadows over its bright green floor, and a merry breeze of sufficient prevalence to emboss each wave with a silvery foam." Coleridge was alone, and Clarke wishing to make himself known to "This genius, the most extraordinary man of his age" walked up to the great man, and introduced himself as a friend of Charles and Mary Lamb. Coleridge accepted the introduction and began a conversation as if they were of long-standing acquaintance.

That morning a girl had thrown herself from the pier-head, in despair from having been badly treated by a man. They spoke about the event, Coleridge denouncing an age when morality hounded the weaker human being from the community and yet still received him who had wronged her. C.C.C. wrote, "We both agreed that the question never will be adjusted, but by the women themselves. Then true to his character Coleridge went onto the great mysteries of life and death, and the sublime question of immortality; and then headlong into the field of ethereal metaphysics. He went on, never pausing for breath for an hour and a half, giving utterance to some of the grandest thoughts I ever heard from the mouth of man. His ideas embodied in words of purest eloquence, flew about my ears like drifts of snow, he was like a cataract filling and rushing over my penny-phial capacity; he required nothing from me, other than my recognition of his discourse."

Keats recalled a similar circumstance in one of his letters to his brother George in 1819. "Last Sunday I took a walk towards Highgate and in the lane that winds by the side of Lord Mansfield's park I met Mr Green our Demonstrator at Guy's in conversation with Coleridge. I joined them, after enquiring by a look whether it would be agreeable. I walked with him at his alderman-after-dinner pace for nearly two miles I suppose. In those two miles he broached a thousand things. Let me see if I can give you a list – Nightingales, Poetry – on Poetical Sensation – Metaphysics – Different genera and species of Dreams – Nightmare – a dream accompanied by a sense of touch – single and double touch – A dream related – First and second consciousness – the difference explained between will and volition – so many metaphysicians from a want of smoking a second consciousness – Monsters – the Kraken – Mermaids – Southey believes in them – Southey's belief too much diluted – A Ghost story – Good morning – I heard his voice as he came towards me, I heard it as he moved away." Benjamin Haydon wrote in his journal that Coleridge said of Keats after shaking his hand that "There was death in that hand."

C.C.C. wrote: "My first suspicion of his being at Ramsgate had arisen from my mother observing that she had heard an elderly gentleman in the public library, who looked like a Dissenting-Minister, talking as she never heard a man talk. Like his own 'Ancient-Mariner' when he had once fixed your eye, he held you spellbound." William Hazlitt once said of him, "He would talk on for ever, and you wished him to talk on for ever." Hazlitt asked Charles Lamb if he had ever heard Coleridge preach? to which Lamb replied, "That he never heard him do anything else."

After Clarke's father's death, his mother and unmarried sister moved from Ramsgate, and went to the West Country to live with the younger sister and her husband. C.C.C. returned to London alone to renew past friendships. One of his first calls was on the Novellos who had moved from Oxford Street to a large old-fashioned property at 8 Percy Street on Stockwell Green. And it was there that he came across the two widows – Mrs Shelley and Mrs Williams – recently returned from Italy after the drowning of their husbands. Vincent and Mary Sabilla Novello were endeavouring, with their friendship and music to help the sad ladies into a calmer life after their shocking bereavements. C.C.C. remembered "Two good-looking women, Mary Wolstonecraft-Godwin-Shelley, with her well shaped, golden haired head, always a little drooping. With her marble white shoulders and arms visible in a plain velvet dress, which she wore low-cut as was the custom of the time, for neither of the women ever put on the widow's cap and weeds." C.C.C., on renewing his visits to the Novellos, found their eldest daughter a grown woman aged sixteen. "Thinking herself grown-up and joining in with the adults' conversation around the supper table."

Towards the end of 1825 Leigh Hunt and his tribe returned from Italy, and the musical evenings resumed as if he had never been away. In 1826 Charles Cowden Clarke visited the Novello home more often. And Mr and Mrs Novello soon realised that the attraction was their eldest daughter. A growing affection between the two blossomed, and they became engaged that year on the first of November. She just seventeen, twenty years younger than Clarke.

Soon after his return to London Charles Clarke went into business as a publisher and bookseller in partnership with Henry Hunt. Clarke for all his education and worldliness was not a man of business and the firm known as Hunt and Clarke failed in 1829, involving William Hazlitt in a loss of £200 on his book *Napoleon*. After his marriage to Mary Victoria Novello, Clarke joined Alfred Novello, her brother, in a music publishing business. Mary, his wife, is best known for her Shakespeare Concordance. Whilst Charles went on to become a well-respected theatre critic and writer of articles on the theatre for the *Atlas* and *Examiner* newspapers. In 1828 he published *Readings in Natural Philosophy*, *Tales from Chaucer* in 1833, and *Adam the Gardener* a book for boys in 1834. In this book he refers to "my old friend Mr Keats" and quotes from his poems. In 1835 came his *The Riches of Chaucer*, in which he gave the account of how Keats came to write 'The Floure and the Lefe' sonnet.

It was about this time that he began his public lectures on Shakespeare and other poets. He was an excellent lecturer, bringing to his teaching skill a very strong voice. He published many of his lectures, and by so doing popularised the study of Shakespeare in the country. When Benjamin Haydon published his biography in 1853, Clarke protested in the *Examiner* of July the 9th about the way that the painter had portrayed Keats. He had accused the poet of 'intemperate habits'. Clarke refused to believe the Cayenne Pepper story (that Keats coated his tongue with pepper to increase sensation when drinking claret). In 1859 Clarke published a volume of his own poetry entitled *Carmina-Minima*. He received recognition for publishing texts on popular British Poets, known as the Gilfillan-Poets. During the latter years of his life he produced together with his wife Mary *The Recollections of Writers*. The couple left England for a warmer climate in 1856 moving to Nice. At Nice they set up home together with Alfred and Sabilla Novello. From the year 1861 they lived in Genoa. Charles Cowden Clarke died on the 13th of March 1877 after a life spanning ninety years. His obituary stated: "Charles Cowden Clarke, beloved and respected, leaves a pleasant memory and a great mass of useful work. And above all the record of a happy and beneficent life."

Mary Victoria Cowden Clarke, lived for another twenty years, continuing to write and publish and republish her own work, and that of her beloved husband. A list of the Works of Charles and Mary Cowden Clarke which covered four pages, appeared in a book by Mary entitled *My Long Life,* second edition 1896. Mary Cowden Clarke died in 1898.

In 1816 Keats wrote three Epistles, the first to George Felton Mathew, the next to 'My Brother George', and then the 'Epistle to Charles Cowden Clarke'. In his lifetime he wrote four of these appraisals for the people that he felt to be at the time his closest friends. The last came two years later, in March 1818 he wrote the 'Epistle to John Hamilton Reynolds'. Included here in its entirety the Clarke epistle:

~ *Epistle to Charles Cowden Clarke* ~

Oft have you seen a swan superbly frowning,
And with proud breast his own white shadow crowning;
He slants his neck beneath the waters bright
So silently, it seems a beam of light
Come from the galaxy: anon he sports, –
With outspread wings the Naiad Zephyr courts,
Or ruffles all the surface of the lake,
In striving from its crystal face to take
Some diamond water drops, and them to treasure
In milky nest, and sip them off at leisure.
But not a moment can he there insure them,
Nor to such downy rest can he allure them;
For down they rush as though they would be free,
And drop like hours into eternity.
Just like that bird am I in loss of time,
Whene'er I venture on the stream of rhyme;
With shatter'd boat, oar snapt, and canvas rent,
I slowly sail, scarce knowing my intent;
Still scooping up the water with my fingers,
In which a trembling diamond never lingers.

By this, friend Charles, you may full plainly see
Why I have never penn'd a line to thee:
Because my thoughts were never free, and clear,

And little fit to please a classic ear;
Because my wine was of too poor a savour
For one whose palate gladdens in the flavour
Of sparkling Helicon: – small good it were
To take him to a desert rude, and bare,
Who had on Baiæ's shore reclin'd at ease,
While Tasso's page was floating in a breeze
That gave soft music from Armida's bowers,
Mingled with fragrance from her rarest flowers:
Small good to one who had by Mulla's stream
Fondled the maidens with the breasts of cream;
Who had beheld Belphœbe in a brook,
And lovely Una in a leafy nook,
And Archimago leaning o'er his book:
Who had of all that's sweet tasted, and seen,
From silv'ry ripple, up to beauty's queen;
From the sequester'd haunts of gay Titania
To the blue dwelling of divine Urania:
One, who, of late had ta'en sweet forest walks
With him who elegantly chats, and talks –
The wrong'd Libertas, – who has told you stories
Of laurel chaplets, and Apollo's glories;
Of troops chivalrous prancing through a city,
And tearful ladies made for love, and pity;
With many else which I have never known.

Thus have I thought; and days on days have flown
Slowly, or rapidly – unwilling still
For you to try my dull, unlearned quill.
Nor should I now, but that I've known you long;
That you first taught me all the sweets of song:
The grand, the sweet, the terse, the free, the fine;
What swell'd with pathos, and what right divine:
Spenserian vowels that elope with ease,
And float along like birds o'er summer seas;
Miltonian storms, and more, Miltonian tenderness.

Michael in arms, and more, meek Eve's fair
slenderness.
Who read for me the sonnet swelling loudly
Up to its climax and then dying proudly?
Who found for me the grandeur of the ode,
Growing, like Atlas, stronger from its load?
Who let me taste that more than cordial dram,
The sharp, the rapier-pointed epigram?
Shew'd me that epic was of all the king,
Round, vast, and spanning all like Saturn's ring?
You too upheld the veil from Clio's beauty,
And pointed out the patriot's stern duty;
The might of Alfred, and the shaft of Tell;
The hand of Brutus, that so grandly fell
Upon a tyrant's head. Ah! had I never seen,
Or known your kindness, what might I have been?
What my enjoyments in my youthful years,
Bereft of all that now my life endears?
And can I e'er these benefits forget?
And can I e'er repay the friendly debt?
No, doubly no; yet should these rhymings please,
I shall roll on the grass with twofold ease;
For I have long time been my fancy feeding
With hopes that you would one day think the reading
Of my rough verses not an hour misspent;
Should it e'er be so, what a rich content!

Some weeks have pass'd since last I saw the spires
In lucent Thames reflected: – warm desires
To see the sun o'erpeep the eastern dimness,
And morning shadows streaking into slimness
Across the lawny fields, and pebbly water;
To mark the time as they grow broad, and shorter;
To feel the air that plays about the hills,
And sips its freshness from the little rills;
To see high, golden corn wave in the light
When Cynthia smiles upon a summer's night,

And peers among the cloudlets jet and white,
As though she were reclining in a bed
Of bean blossoms, in heaven freshly shed –
No sooner had I stepp'd into these pleasures,
Than I began to think of rhymes and measures:
The air that floated by me seem'd to say
"Write! thou wilt never have a better day."
And so I did. When many lines I'd written,
Though with their grace I was not oversmitten,
Yet, as my hand was warm, I thought I'd better
Trust to my feelings, and write you a letter.
Such an attempt required an inspiration
of a peculiar sort, – a consummation; –
Which, had I felt, these scribblings might have been
Verses from which the soul would never wean;
But many days have passed since last my heart
Was warm'd luxuriously by divine Mozart;
By Arne delighted, or by Handel madden'd;
Or by the song of Erin pierc'd and sadden'd:
What time you were before the music sitting,
And the rich notes to each sensation fitting.
Since I have walk'd with you through shady lanes
That freshly terminate in open plains,
And revel'd in a chat that ceased not
When at nightfall among your books we got:
No, nor when supper came, nor after that, –
Nor when reluctantly I took my hat;
No, nor till cordially you shook my hand
Midway between our homes: – your accents bland
Still sounded in my ears, when I no more
Could hear your footsteps touch the grav'ly floor
Sometimes I lost them, and then found again;
You chang'd the footpath for the grassy plain.
In those still moments I have wish'd you joys
That well you know to honour: – "Life's very toys,
"With him", said I, "will take a pleasant charm;
"It cannot be that ought will work him harm".

These thoughts now come o'er me with all their might:
Again I shake your hand, – friend Charles, good-night.

John Keats, September 1816

PART II

Charles Armitage-Brown
1787–1842

On the fourteenth of April 1787, at Lambeth London, in a big lonely family house that stood in Grays Walk. Jane Brown wife of William, gave birth to her sixth son. Named Charles, he was christened at the parish church of Lambeth on August the 25th. Charles was the youngest in the large family, but in eighteenth-century London his childhood was far from sheltered. His father was often away from home, working in the city as a broker. His eldest brother John was a merchant in London. Another brother, Henry, sailed the tropics as a midshipman. At home the young Charles was required to take his turn as man of the house, and defender of the family's property. For reasons that were likely to have been economic he was not sent to a public school. His early education took place at a good local school run by a clergyman. Little is known of his education beyond that time. Later on at school he met with Charles Wentworth Dilke and the two became firm friends; a friendship lasting well into their adult lives.

Dilke's father was clerk at the Admiralty office and to the young Brown became almost a second father. The closeness of the families and their love of literature formed the mould for an enduring friendship.

At school Brown began his study of Shakespeare, and developed a firm working knowledge of the writer, a knowledge and enthusiasm that he would later pass on to John Keats.

But in the age of industrial revolution in a hard middle-class competitive world, there was little time for further education.

And he left his schooling at the age of fourteen, to take up employment with a firm of accountants. Having gained some knowledge of business, he joined his brother John in the mercantile profession. John had had some success in London and resolved to work on his own account. Going to Russia he set up an office in St Petersburg. He was soon able to offer his younger brother Charles, now aged eighteen, a position within the company. Accepting, Charles crossed a continent to join him. He wrote of his arrival, "At last we came to the gates of St Petersburg a high triumphal arch. We were wheeled up to my brother's house where he received me most cordially, and I found myself again completely installed in the duties of a counting house. After the first welcome nothing was talked of, even during supper, but the prices of tallow, hemp, flax and bristles." His days were filled with work and there was little free time to explore the great city. He gives us some idea of his experiences when in later life he wrote *Walter Hazlebourn*. The love interest in the book, *Fidalma-Vivaldi*, was probably based on his own first love, Miss Kennedy, the daughter of a governess to the Grand Duke Michael, who sadly disappointed him when she deserted Charles for a wealthy English merchant, who later died a bankrupt. Years after she tried to revive the love affair but Charles had suffered too much at her hands to forget or forgive her. When he wrote *Walter Hazlebourn* a work that he failed to finish, he meets Fidalma again in Florence. In the book, Brown always a romantic, makes his hero leave his wife to live with her.

The Russian adventure during which he suffered rejection by Miss Kennedy also included his brother's business failure. In 1807 The Russians secretly signed a treaty 'The Treaty of Tilsit' in which they agreed to assist France in a commercial war against England. This was a disaster for John Armitage Brown, and his business failed. Now at the age of twenty, Charles Brown recrossed the Baltic for England and home.

This setback was quickly followed by heartache; two of his brothers died prematurely. His father took to drink, went mad and died in an asylum. He left his family a sizeable fortune and they would have been comfortably off except that the widow soon found a second husband – Joseph Rennoit Browne, a man hated by the surviving siblings. It was some time before the family found that the stepfather was secretly dissipating their fortune.

Whatever Brown's disappointments, the time spent at St Petersburg proved worthwhile. In 1809 he wrote *Narensky*, or *The Road to Yaroslaf* a comic opera based on his Russian adventures. Accepted for Drury Lane it was performed there in 1814. He must have felt a deal of pleasure when he read on January 11th 1814 the announcement in *The Times* advertising the play, he first literary success. Brown received payment of £300 and a silver ticket that gave him free admission to Drury Lane theatre for life. *Narensky* was only on stage ten times and then reduced to just two acts. Brown, independent as usual, declared that he had received much more than the opera was worth, and destroyed every copy of the libretto he could find.

Now in his middle-twenties Charles was a disillusioned businessman. However he had gained some knowledge of the literary world, he now longed to be accepted into the company of literate men. Now he became an agent for his brother James of the East India Company. Then James became ill and in May 1815 returned to England. In October of the same year he died at the age of thirty-five. It was rumoured that he had been poisoned by a disgruntled native servant.

The death of James brought Charles financial security, with a legacy of £10,000 and a share of an estate at Lambeth.

It was at this opportune moment that the friend of his schooldays, Charles Wentworth Dilke now working at the Navy Pay Office in London, approached Brown with his idea of building a country cottage that they both could share. The following month, November 1815, under their joint supervision, the builders began work on a house in Hampstead, that would later be known as Wentworth Place.

In 1816 Brown moved into his part of the bright new house.

Hampstead, with its heath and air like wine was a joy to him, and was to fulfil his desire for the company of literary men. Leigh Hunt was a near neighbour, and visitors to his Vale of Health Cottage were Thomas Barnes, the Editor of the *Times*, Vincent Novello, the famed organist, Bejamin Haydon, the egocentric painter of huge historic pictures, an exhibitor at the Royal Academy and supporter of the Elgin Marbles. Among the literary men were John Hamilton Reynolds the young poet lawyer, William Hazlitt, critic and lecturer and the poet Percy Bysshe Shelley. Brown was soon accepted within this hallowed group as a genuine wit of his time.

It was not however at Wentworth Place or on the Vale of Health, but on the Hampstead Road, late in the summer of 1817 that Brown first met a youth of twenty-one with "the hazel eyes of a wild gypsy, set in the face of a god".

"In that interview of a minute," he wrote, "I inwardly desired his acquaintance, if not his friendship." The smallest detail of the first meeting with Keats remained in his memory to the end of his life.

This chance meeting with Brown would be for Keats the beginning of a more settled time in his troubled life for he had never felt domestically secure. And now, having given up all his training in the medical profession to follow his love of poetry, he really needed encouragement and support from someone with a mind like that of Brown's. Richard Abbey the tea merchant and guardian of the Keats' family fortunes, had encouraged John in the pursuit of a career in the medical profession. But now Keats had abandoned all he had worked for on what seemed to Abbey just a foolish whim. This was to the staid businessman, madness. And so it must have seemed to those who had instructed him, bringing him to a level where he was able to pass a difficult examination obtaining a licence with which he could practise as an Apothecary (one who could make up and dispense medicines). Abbey railed on him, "John, half your fortune spent and for what?" Abbey has been reviled by many biographers for his philistine insensitivity, but his anger at this time is completely understandable. Now both his insecurity and indecision made the meeting on the Hampstead road the more momentous. For Brown, also with a troubled background, had given up a solid profession in commerce in favour of literature. In the more worldly wise and genial older man, Keats found the companion that he needed. In Keats, Brown recognised one whose wit and depth of mind he had never come across before. He believed that there stood before him a superior being. Afterwards Brown wrote, "Everyone who met him, sought his society. I succeeded in making him come often to my house by never asking him to come oftener. And I let him feel himself at perfect liberty there, chiefly by avoiding to assure him of the fact. We quickly became intimate."

By the autumn Keats was visiting Brown on successive days for dinner. December saw them going to the Drury Lane Theatre, Brown using his silver ticket.

In January 1818 Keats began to work at Wentworth Place, sitting by the fire in Brown's parlour copying out his poems late into the night. He told his friends, "I am a good deal with Brown and Dilke, we are very thick."

On the 22nd of June 1818, having let out his half of Wentworth Place for the summer, Brown left town with Keats on a walking tour of the Lake District and Scottish Highlands. They took a coach as far as Liverpool, accompanied by George Keats and his new wife. Here they bade farewell to the couple that were sailing for America, and Charles Brown saw himself taking the place of a lost brother.

As they travelled, Brown wrote in his journal to minute every detail of the journey. John in a letter to his brother Tom.

"Each evening Brown pulls from his knapsack; 1st his paper – then his pens, and last his ink, now I say, why not take out his pens first sometimes. But I might as well tell a hen to hold up her head before she drinks instead of afterwards."

Brown's writings were much more than a fad, more than a desire to describe his holidays to a friend. For the friends of Keats all had a personal interest in all that concerned him. They preserved his letters, copied his poetry, noted the slightest incidents of his life, conscious in some way that they were in the presence of genius. "Who am I?" asked Brown. "Not one that can share the transports of his imagination, but a humble plodding man, a commonplace fellow who had the foresight to carry with him pens and paper, and the wilful industry to write and sketch all he saw and all he felt." Brown began to understand even then that he must be a Boswell. He also gave assistance to the poet's muse. One day close to the path, he said, "it's here no doubt that Old Meg Merrilies had often boiled her kettle, and perhaps cooked a chicken. While finishing our breakfast both employed at our writing, I could not avoid noticing that Keats' letter was not running in regular prose. He told me he was writing to his little sister, and giving a ballad on Old Meg for her amusement. Though he called it too much a trifle to be copied I soon inserted it in my journal." Twenty-two years later he would recall his "Walks in the North" for *The Plymouth and Devonport Weekly Journal.* Then, on August the 7th he wrote from Inverness to Charles Dilke's nephew, John Snook, the Bedhampton Millers son. "Mr Keats will leave me here, I am full of sorrow about it. He is not well enough to go on; a violent cold and an ulcerated throat make it a matter of prudence that he should return to London."

Twelve days later, at Wentworth Place, Maria Dilke recorded: "John Keats arrived here last night, as brown and as shabby as you can imagine. Scarcely any shoes left, his jacket all torn at the back, a fur cap, a great plaid, and his knapsack. I cannot tell what he looked like!" He returned to a first meeting with Fanny Brawne, for it was to her mother that Charles Brown had let Wentworth Place for the summer. It was Brown who was indirectly responsible for the Brawnes' decision to settle in Hampstead, and for Keats' introduction to the attractive eighteen-year-old daughter.

Tom Keats, John's younger brother lay seriously ill in the final stages of tuberculosis at their lodging with the Bentleys at Well Walk. On the first of December he died. Keats walked in a daze of exhaustion to his friend at Wentworth Place. Brown said, "I awoke to find him standing silently beside my bed. I instinctively reached for his hand, and requested that he would come and live with me, as now apart from his sister at Walthamstow he had to my knowledge no living relative in England."

In mid December Keats moved from Well Walk to Wentworth Place to lodge with Brown, paying an agreed figure of £5 a month. Brown was completely devoted to Keats and it was never just a business arrangement. Brown was happy to offer Keats the security and companionship he needed. He included John in his busy social life in an effort to take his mind off the loss of Tom. Brown, it seems, knew nothing of his young friend's love affair with the beautiful Mrs Isabella Jones whom the poet had been seeing for the past six months (see Isabella's story within Peter Davey's book *A Poet in Love*). Keats kept his promise that he would not mention her name to any of their acquaintances. Brown had an invitation to spend Christmas with Charles Dilke's parents at Chichester, an invitation that was extended to Keats. Brown left town for Chichester just before Christmas, but Keats, again suffering with a sore throat put off the travelling.

Keats nursed his sore throat. And spent some time with the indulgent Isabella Jones over the two weeks before leaving London for Chichester and Brown.

In mid-January (date unknown) Keats stayed the night in town at Isabella's apartment. Early in the morning of the following day he boarded the fast coach for Chichester where Brown met him as the coach deposited its passengers at the Inn. They walked together from the centre of City to the East Gate and the elderly Dilkes. The evenings were spent playing cards with dowager widow ladies, acquaintances of their hosts. Keats explored the rich architecture of the eleventh-century cathedral, and the octagonal market cross. And as he sat in the third floor attic bedroom with a view from its window of the city and pastures beyond, he began work on his new poem 'The Eve of St Agnes'.

On the 23rd of January 1819, on a fine but windy day Keats and Brown set off to walk the thirteen miles to Bedhampton. They were to stay for a time at the Mill House with the miller John Snook and his wife Letitia, sister of Charles Dilke of Hampstead. Brown said they enjoyed a little religion, politics, and talk on farming. Keats asked John Snook to write down anything that he thought might be of use to his brother George on the subject of farming.

One day they borrowed Snook's pony and trap to travel the few miles to Stansted House where Mr Way was consecrating his Chapel there to the conversion of Jews. They arrived late and had to stand in a draughty entrance. The cold was to bring on yet another sore throat for the poet. Brown returned to Hampstead, leaving his friend behind for a few days of recuperation in the care of Letitia Snook. Keats sat in his bedroom at the rear of the Mill-House overlooking the saltings, breathing the clean air and putting the finishing touches to his poem. The poem was full of Chichester, Stansted House and Isabella Jones. Keats wrote to George in America, "I went to Chichester and Bedhampton, nothing worth speaking of happened at either place. I wrote a little poem called St Agnes Eve." Early in February Brown and Keats were at home in Hampstead, and the poet found himself caught up in Brown's busy social life.

They went with Leigh Hunt to Vincent Novello's for musical entertainment, cheese and Lutheran Beer. Hunt's behaviour seems again to have upset Keats, for later he wrote to George. "I promise myself I will have no more of it." Brown began flirting with Fanny Brawne and wrote a Valentine for her. Keats was put out; but as his friend had no idea of John's interest in the girl he had little to complain about.

Keats wrote of further social engagements; they had tea with the Dilkes on the 9th birthday of their son Charley. Brown gave a party for Burridge Davenport, a merchant friend from Church Row who came with Miss Winter, Miss Barnes and the children. He entertained Joseph Severn the painter, and John Cawthorn, the bookseller to the Prince of Wales and publisher of *Narensky*.

There were, however less pleasant happenings. In April Brown's little nephews arrived to stay for the Easter holidays. "They have been a toothache to me," Keats wrote, "Their voices are like wasp stings." To make up for the inconvenience Brown gave, as he said a "Claret Feast", knowing John's fondness for the wine. Charles Dilke came, John Hamilton Reynolds was there, Brown's solicitor Robert Skinner came with Mancur the mysterious man of letters. Brown's brother John Armitage arrived, still an energetic man of business. Lastly John Martin the publisher who had sold Brown's comic opera. All company that Brown cherished. Keats thoroughly enjoyed himself, the wine flowed freely and most of the eight in the party became a little inebriated. Brown now enjoyed an easy lifestyle without money worries, he could well afford to entertain his literary friends. He was now absorbed in literature. He could recognise great writers of the past and present without looking up the title pages.

Little of Brown's own writing of this period has been found. It's likely that about this time his work began to appear in Colburn's *New Monthly Magazine*. What can be deduced is that his writings were thought to be genial and earthy. "Brown and I," said Keats, "sit opposite one another all day authorising." In the small parlour at Wentworth Place, he paced up and down as Keats said "breeding – now at this moment he is being delivered of a couplet – and I dare say it will be as well as can be expected – Gracious, he has twins!"

In his next letter to George and Georgiana in America, Keats sent a mocking word portrait of Brown:

He is weet a melancholy Carle:
Thin in waist, with bushy head of hair,
As hath the seeded thistle when in parle
It holds the Zephyr ere it sendeth fair
Its light balloons into the summer air;
Therto his beard had not begun to bloom,
No brush had touch'd his chin or razor sheer;
No care has touch'd his cheek with mortal doom,
But new he was and bright as scarf from Persian loom.

Ne cared he for wine, or half and half
Ne cared he for fish or flesh or fowl,
And sauces held he worthless as the chaff;
He's deign'd the swine herd at the wassail bowl;
Ne with lewd ribbalds sat he cheek by jowl;
Ne with sly Lemans in the scorner's chair;
But after water brooks his Pilgrim's soul
Panted, and all his food was woodland air
Though he would oft times feast on gilliflowers rare.

The slang of cities in no wise he knew,
Tipping the wink to him was heathen Greek;
He sipp'd no olden Tom or ruin blue,
Or nantz or cherry-brandy drank full meek
By many a damsel hoarse and rouge of cheek;
Nor did he know each aged watchman's beat,

Nor in obscured purlieus would he seek
For curled Jewesses, with ankles neat,
Who as they walk abroad make tinkling with their feet.

With the memory of his Scottish adventure still fresh, Keats seems to be unsuccessfully using some of the dialect. To understand this poem, one must turn it into opposites. For Brown had little hair on his head, he had a penchant for both wine and women, and was known to be extremely earthy in his humour. In the spring of 1819 Charles and Maria Dilke moved out of Wentworth Place, Dilke, in spite of his radical views, and Brown's condemnation of the fagging system in the great schools, had decided to send his son as a day boy to Westminster. The Dilkes moved to Great Smith Street in the City so as to be nearer the school.

Mrs Brawne had arranged beforehand to take up permanent residence in Hampstead; and as the Dilkes moved out Mrs Brawne, a widow in her early thirties, moved in with her family of three children – Fanny eighteen, Samuel fourteen and Margaret aged nine.

And now with Fanny close by next-door, John's feelings for her grew. Brown's continued flirting sent the poet into a whirl of indecision, torn between his now best friend and the girl he was beginning to fall in love with. Despite these complications within his life he was about to enter into what would prove to be, the most prolific few months of his poetic genius.

In April he wrote the sonnet 'La Belle Dame Sans Merci', the sonnet 'To Sleep', the first of the great odes, 'The Ode to Psyche' and in May came 'The Ode on a Grecian Urn'.

He composed without a thought on fame and public acceptance of his work. He wrote, caring not if the poems of a day would be destroyed by the next morning. It was Charles Brown who rescued the discarded scraps of paper, Brown who saved 'The Ode to a Nightingale' from certain destruction. Brown said, "he gave me permission to copy any verses that he might write, and I fully availed myself of it.

He cared so little for them himself when once his imagination was released." What a blessing it was that Brown in his wisdom made himself responsible for saving the poet's work.

In May they planned a tour of the continent together, but had to abandon the idea for lack of funds. Keats was almost broke and was so unsettled that he considered picking up with his early profession as an Apothecary, for which his licence was still valid. He even discussed with Brown an idea that came to him, that he would go to sea, to take up a position as a surgeon on an Indiaman. Brown was horrified, and again used his foresight. He loaned Keats enough money for his immediate needs, and managed to turn his mind away from these wild schemes. However even then Keats had thoughts of trying to write for the press once more. In the following two months Keats wrote that Brown and he "harnessed themselves to their dogcart versifying." Brown copied Drayton's tribute to the power of fairy tales, and began his own title 'Faries Triumph' which he never finished, its only importance being that it was a combined production by Brown and Keats:

Shed no tear, – O Shed no tear!
The flower will bloom another year;
Weep no more, – O weep no more!
Young buds sleep in the root's white core;
Dry your eyes, – O dry your eyes!
For I was taught in Paradise
To ease the heart in melodies–
            Shed no tear!

Over-head – look overhead,
'Mong the blossoms white and red;
Look up, look up – I flutter now
On this flush pomegranate bough;
See me – 'tis this silvery bill
Ever cures the good man's ill.

Shed no tear – O shed no tear!
The flower will bloom another year.
Adieu, – adieu – I fly, adieu!
I vanish in the heaven's blue –
                    Adieu, adieu!

And so on, and so on! Keats soon lost interest. And Brown abandoned the work when the summer came. James Rice, a good and long-standing friend who had suffered indifferent health for most of his life, suggested that both he and Keats take a holiday together for the summer. The Isle of Wight was put forward as a suitable destination, to which Keats readily agreed.

On June the 27th they took the night coach to Portsmouth, Keats again riding on the outside. He had left his winter coat in Hampstead and suffered from the chill of the night air. On arrival, it's hard to say which of the two friends had suffered the most. John records that he felt restless and unwell, with the onset again of his sore throat. He complains that the poor health of his friend only made his own predicament the greater.

Charles Brown found a tenant for his part of Wentworth Place for the summer and set off to be with Keats. John Martin the publisher joined the party and the four played at cards into the early hours. James Rice left with Martin in company for London and home, leaving Brown and Keats to concentrate on higher things. Keats began 'Lamia', Brown walked and sketched, he lent Keats paper and pencils, and the two enjoyed a light-hearted competition on who could produce the better drawing.

One evening as John sat dreaming Brown drew his portrait. It was a delicate pencilled profile that caught the poet's likeness to perfection. Brown had gone above his skill to produce an excellent and inspired work.

The idea of writing a play came into Brown's mind, and the two collaborated to produce *Otho the Great*. Brown provided the plot and Keats produced the dialogue. They hoped it might be good enough for Edmund Kean the Shakespearean actor to perform at Drury Lane. Later that year Brown offered it to both Drury Lane and Covent Garden but on each occasion the manuscript was returned. As Brown said, "unopened and unread". Unfortunately Brown had taken Keats back to the adolescent writing style that he had long since given up.

Brown went off walking the countryside, leaving Keats to concentrate on more laudable work. Still with the thought of some success with play-writing. Keats began *King Stephen* which may have indeed reached the stage had he ever finished it. On August the 12th the pair left the Isle of Wight for the mainland and Winchester. Keats noted in a letter to George a happening during the crossing from the Isle of Wight to the mainland. He commented on the imperturbable behaviour of the officers and men on board a naval craft that had almost collided with their own vessel. In the same letter he described accurately the Prince Regent's new yacht as it rode at anchor at Cowes. Winchester delighted Keats; Brown said the City was like Oxford, but situated among hills. "There were trees, streams of clear water, old buildings, the pleasantest town I ever was in." The clear air over the chalky subterranean was as John said "worth sixpence a pint" and his sore throat began to improve immediately. The friends had expected to find a decent library, but were disappointed. However the city was full of good book shops. Brown read in a local newspaper of Edmund Kean's plans to go to America and shelved *Otho the Great* until the next season. For the same reason Keats thought that there was no point in continuing with his *King Stephen*. He had already been put out when Brown, reading the part he had written suggested some changes to the plot; "Stop! stop!" he cried, "I have already been too long in leading strings, I will do this myself." Kean then abandoned his plan to go to America, but by then Keats had moved on to other works.

At this time both Brown and Keats had serious financial problems. Brown who depended on quarterly and half-yearly receipts from his investments had been lending money to John all year and was not at all flush. Keats, waiting on repayment of his loans to Benjamin Haydon, was to be again disappointed. He had made loans of £230 which he could ill afford to have done. Richard Abbey had warned him of a possible Chancery suit and would advance no further money. By September, in fear of debtors' prison in Winchester with but a few shillings left, he wrote to Taylor in desperation. The publisher was away on holiday and failed to reply but Hessey his partner sent £30. Brown borrowed another £30 from a Hampshire friend, further funds came from an amount left at the Chichester post office. They were solvent, and the threat of jail averted! Brown left Keats in Winchester, to give as he said, "John a time of solitude to concentrate on new poems" and went off to Chichester to visit with the Dilkes and Snooks.

Keats on his own, decided that he would not return to Hampstead and Fanny Brawne. He felt that his feelings for her were smothering and he wanted to free himself from his dependence on Brown.

During his lonely stay in Chichester, Brown thought about past great men of letters. Burns, and his cottage at Dumfries 'That abode of unhappiness', Shakespeare's tomb at Stratford that he and Keats had visited just a year before. But Brown was not one to harbour melancholy. "I never went into Collin's house at the corner of Chichester Cloisters; how melancholy it looks. Often I stood before it, with as little desire to pass the threshold as to enter his grave." He was brought back to the problems of the living when a strange letter arrived from Keats. The poet said that he had decided not to return to Wentworth Place and Hampstead. In this stiff and rather churlish letter he intimated that he wished to wean himself both from his friend and benefactor and from close contact with Fanny Brawne. Brown leaving his Chichester hosts hurried to board a coach and returned to Winchester. In his heart he knew that Keats could not escape his feelings for Fanny. Inflexible, Keats would not be diverted from his plan. In October they returned to London, Keats to a lodging in Westminster which Dilke had found near to his own home. Brown went back to Wentworth Place. Ann, his servant of long standing, had left during the summer, and before departing had recommended her friend Abigail O'Donaghue for the vacant position. Abigail, a young Irish woman of striking appearance, was installed as a live-in servant. Brown was soon attracted to the girl, and began a relationship that went way beyond that of master and maid. But their relationship became of minor importance, for just as Brown had surmised the poet's second try at separation and solitude had failed. Two days after settling at College Street Westminster he turned up at Wentworth Place searching for Fanny. In spite of what had gone before, and being upset by his strange, bitter, accusing letters of the summer she received him lovingly. Within the week he had decided to return to Hampstead (see Peter Davey's book *A Poet in Love* for Fanny Browne's story).

Keats returned with a troubled mind; worried about money, his brother George's problems in America, uncertainty about Fanny, a persistent sore throat and feeling weak, these the first signs of consumption. Abigail found a bottle of laudanum and he admitted to Brown that he had been taking it. Brown persuaded Keats to give up the dangerous medication. Keats promised; but it was a promise that would be broken, for he had been taking it for some months and would secretly continue to do so. Keats developed an unnatural antagonism against the world and those about him. He was restless and suffering from mood swings, all likely caused by a growing tubercular infection. His friends noted how he would argue and disagree over the smallest of things, things that before he would have laughed at. He wrote to his brother George complaining of Leigh Hunt's puns and piano playing; Haydon's grand ideas, and his continually trying to borrow money; Charles Dilke's way of always being in the right, if Dilke thought that white was indeed black then so be it. He railed against the Reynolds sisters for their dullness and jealousies. Things that at one time would have amused him now tried his temper. When Abigail O'Donaghue said that an engraving of Shakespeare reminded her of her father, Keats was enraged. One night when dining in town he overheard a group of artists criticising Joseph Severn's painting. Severn had just been awarded a Gold Medal by the Academy. He rose from the table in a rage, saying, "I will not sit at table with such snobs and liars." His despair with his fellow man seemed complete when he wrote to Georgiana his sister-in-law in America, "Standing at Charing Cross and looking East, West, North and South I see nothing but dullness. Upon the whole I dislike mankind."

His brother George arrived at Wentworth Place in the first week of January 1820. In financial difficulty he had returned to England in an effort to raise as much money as he could, claiming his share of the late Tom's estate. What took place during his three-week stay would alienate him from some of the poet's friends for many years. (The rights and wrongs of the matter were to be debated over time.) Fanny Brawne would say, "He is no favourite of mine, and never liked me." Brown said, "I hate what George has done to John." But during George's stay in England the brothers remained on amicable terms, and it was only after George's departure and his return to America that Keats remarked to Brown, "George should not have done that." However his disappointment did not last, for he continued writing to his brother without a hint of animosity.

Brown was soon disturbed by further signs of John's melancholy; he noticed that the poet had given up writing 'The Cap and Bells' and no longer made any pretence of revising 'Hyperion'. Worse was soon to come. The long spell of wintry weather broke, and the month of February set in warmer. During the winter Dr Sawbry had advised Brown to get Keats a new warmer topcoat, but now Keats had put the greatcoat aside although the nights were still cold. On the night of Thursday the 3rd of February he came back at eleven o'clock from town, riding on the outside of the coach for its cheapness. The chill night wind cut him to the bone. He staggered the few hundred yards from the stop at Pond Street in a fever and arrived at the door of Wentworth Place stumbling like a drunk. Brown saw at once that his friend was seriously ill and immediately sent him upstairs to bed. As Brown came into the bedroom bringing a glass of spirits, Keats was just getting between the bed sheets. As he did so, he coughed; it was the slightest of coughs, but Brown heard him say "That is blood from my mouth." He was examining a single drop of blood upon the sheet. As Brown came forward, he said, "Charles bring me the candle that I may see this blood." They both stared at it; then looking up with a steady calm which Brown would never forget, he said, "I know the colour of that blood; it is arterial blood. I cannot be deceived in that colour. That drop of blood is my death warrant, I must die."

Brown's account of what took place exactly describes a small lung haemorrhage. Later that night further coughing enlarged the area of bleeding, and such a rush of blood came to Keats' mouth that he thought he might suffocate. He felt that he was dying, and could only gasp out to Brown, "This is unfortunate." This was a typical Keats' understatement and bore no relation to his real feelings at the time.

"Mr Keats fell very ill yesterday week," Brown wrote in his letter to John Snook on February the 11th. "My office of head nurse has too much employed me to allow of my answering your letter immediately. He is somewhat better but I'm in a very anxious state about him."

In March, Keats in a highly nervous condition suffered a nightmare, Brown heard him singing. He was too weak to leave his bed and too troubled to read letters. Brown sent to town for Dr Robert Bree a specialist in disease of the lungs, who had before attended to Keats' brother Tom. Dr Bree declared, despite all evidence to the contrary, that there was no disease in his patient's lungs. Abigail O'Donaghue in Brown's bed disturbed the wakeful Keats with her noisy lovemaking. He was upset by the inconsiderate behaviour of his friend, but also jealous that Brown was able to enjoy something that he himself wished to have with Fanny, living just a few yards from his room. Keats, like all consumptives and those with complaints of the lung, had developed a quickened sense of imagination.

Towards the end of March it seemed as if at last some vestige of health was returning. He gained enough strength to walk out in the spring sunshine over Hampstead Heath, and the doctor even suggested another Scottish walk. Keats knew that the hardships of such a venture would be too much in his fragile state. Abigail was now pregnant with Brown's child, and left Hampstead at his request to return to her home in Ireland. In April Brown let out his half of the house for the summer, two months earlier than normal. His usual practice was to rent out the rooms from the beginning of June. But now Brown had other things on his mind – Abigail and his unborn child, his own and Keats' shortage of money. The doctor had told him that there was no reason to believe that Keats might not make a full recovery. This reassurance proved to be wrong, but there is no way Brown would have known what the near future was to hold.

Keats moved out of Wentworth Place to a lodging in Kentish Town, a lodging found for him by Leigh Hunt very near to his own home; that he might more easily watch over his sick friend. Brown paid a week's rent in advance and borrowed some money from his lawyer Mr Skynner, £50 of which he lent to Keats for his own use. On the 7th of May the two friends sailed together on a smack as far as Gravesend, where they parted company never to meet again. Brown set off for a holiday in Scotland and Keats returned to his lodging in Kentish Town. Did Brown sail directly to Scotland or did he in fact go to Ireland and Abigail O'Donaghue? We know that he went through a Catholic marriage ceremony about that time. A marriage that would not have been recognised in England. Little is known of the event for he never spoke of it, only to confirm that his child did not enter the world as a bastard. A boy child was born later that year that Brown named Carlino.

It is hard to explain how Brown could force Keats to move to strange lodgings alone in his delicate state of health. But his own private affairs were pressing, he was also short of money and had to rent his house out early to raise funds. And the doctors had told him that Keats was progressing towards recovery.

Keats' first letter to Brown written on the 15th of May gives no hint of the collapse to come, except that he seemed not to be enjoying his new lodgings:

To Charles Brown, (15th May 1920)
My Dear Brown,
    You must not expect me to date my letter from such a place as this: you have heard the name; that is sufficient, except merely to tell you it is the 15th instant. You know I was very well in the smack; I have continued much the same, and am well enough to extract much more pleasure than pain out of the summer, even though I should get no better. I shall not say a word about the stanza you promised yourself through my medium, and will swear, at some future time, I promised. Let us hope I may send you more in my next.

The fragment of the letter is all that Brown gave to the biographer, Monkton Milnes, about the letter he says:

"It was his choice during my absence, to lodge at Kentish Town, that he might be near his friend Leigh Hunt, in whose companionship he was ever happy. He went with me in the Scottish smack as far as Gravesend. This was on the 7th of May. I never saw him afterwards. As evidence of his well-being I had requested him to send me some new stanzas to his comic faery poem; for, since his illness, he had not dared the exertion of composing. At the end of eight days he wrote in good spirits."

Keats' statement upon not dating the letter must have been to tease Brown who was strict in such matters.

Sometime in the June Keats wrote a longer letter, still not mentioning the relapse that was almost upon him. These letters were now beginning to follow Brown walking in Scotland.

To Charles Brown. (June 1820)
My Dear Brown,

I have only been to Dilke's once since you left, when we could not find your letters. [The original letter did not name Dilke, but Brown sent all his letters from Scotland to Dilke for distribution.] Now this is bad of me, I should in this instance, conquer the great aversion to breaking up my regular habits, which grows upon me more and more. True, I have an excuse in the weather, which drives one from shelter to shelter in any little excursion. I have not heard from George.

My book is coming out with very low hopes, [the publication of the new poems, Lamia – Isabella etc.] though not in spirits on my part. This shall be my last trial; not succeeding, I shall try what I can do in the apothecary line. When you hear from or see Taylor it is probable you will hear some complaints against me, which this notice is not intended to forestall. The fact is I did behave badly; but it is to be attributed to my health, spirits, and the disadvantageous ground I stand in society. I could go and accommodate matters if I were not too weary of the world. I know that they are more happy and comfortable than I am; therefore why should I trouble myself about it?

I foresee I shall know very few people in the course of a year or two. Men get such different habits that they become as oil and vinegar to one another. Thus far I have consciousness of having been pretty dull and heavy, both in subject and phase; I might add, enigmatically. I am in the wrong, and the world is in the right, I have no doubt. Fact is, I have had so many kindnesses done me by so many people, that I am 'cheveaux-de-frised' with benefits, which I must jump over or break down. I met Monkhouse [Thomas Monkhouse, a relation of Wordsworth] in town a few days ago, who invited me to supper to meet Wordsworth, Southey, Lamb, Haydon, and some more. [Crabb Robinson records an evening spent at Monkhouse's on the 21st of June 1820] I was too careful of my health to risk being out at night. Talking of that, I continue to improve slowly, but I think, surely.

All the talk at present. There is a famous exhibition in Pall-Mall [At the British Institution in June 1820. Portraits of James the 1st, George the 2nd and Devereux] of the old English portraits by Vandyck and Holbein, Sir Peter Lely, and the great Sir Godfrey. Pleasant countenances predominate; so I will mention two or three unpleasant ones. There is James the First, whose appearance would disgrace a "Society for the Suppression of Women" so very squalid and subdued to nothing he looks. Then there is old Lord Burleigh the high priest of economy, the political save all, who has the appearance of a Pharisee just rebuffed by a Gospel (bon-mot). Then there is George the Second, very like an unintellectual Voltaire, troubled with the gout and a bad temper. Then, there is young Devereux, the favourite, with every appearance of as slang a boxer as any in the Court; his face is cast in the mould of Blackguardism with jockey-plaster. I shall soon begin upon 'Lucy Vaughan Lloyd'.[The pen name that Keats intended to use to publish 'The Cap and Bells.] When I have sent off this, I shall write another to some place about fifty miles in advance of you.

Good morning to you.

Yours ever sincerely
John Keats

By July Keats was very ill, his doctor warned that another English winter would probably kill him. And towards the end of August as the days were growing cool, his friends gathered to discuss sending him to Italy. Brown himself made his way from one post office to another, vainly looking for letters. But it was not until September the 9th, at Dunkeld, that he found a batch of correspondence; among the letters were two from Wentworth Place. Brown turned around to make his way homeward.

On the night of the 17th of September a Scottish smack anchored off Gravesend, Brown was onboard eager to return to Wentworth Place for news of Keats. Unknown to him and to the passenger on a brigantine moored within hailing distance. Keats was on board the *Maria Crowther* beginning his voyage to Italy. Finding the Brawnes at Wentworth Place in a state of distress and having missed Keats' departure by just a day, Brown set off for Chichester to spend a month with the elderly Dylkes. Brown has been accused by biographers of deliberately delaying his return to London to avoid going with Keats to Italy. There is no evidence that he did, and there was no way he could have known that Keats' health would deteriorate so suddenly. For just three months before the doctors had told him otherwise, and Keats' letters of June gave the impression of one in good spirits and getting well again.

Even if Charles Brown had avoided the responsibility, who could have blamed him? He had a new wife to support with a child soon to be born, no time to go traipsing off to Italy.

Also he was very short of money, and could not have paid for the passage of Keats and himself to Italy. As it happened Taylor and others had put up the funds, and sent an amount to a Rome deposit for the living costs of both Keats and Severn. If Brown himself had undertaken the mission, is it likely that the same people would have funded it?

The last letter from Wentworth Place to Brown was the one that sent him hurrying on his return to London, this letter was probably written on the 20th of August. (No address or postmark recorded.)

To Charles Brown. [Sunday 20th Aug: 1820?]
My Dear Brown,
        You may not have heard from [Dilke or Hunt] or in anyway, [The names are blanked out on the copy of this letter, and have been inserted as being likely.] that an attack of spitting blood, and all its weakening consequences, has prevented me from writing for so long a time. I have matter now for a very long letter, but no news: so I must cut everything short. I shall make some confession, which you will be the only person for many reasons I shall trust with. [Just what this confession was is not known, for Brown never revealed what Keats had told him in this letter, he took its secrets with him to his grave. Keats might just have unburdened himself about the possible venereal infection that he had suffered with for some time.]
        A winter in England would, I have no doubt, kill me; so I have resolved to go to Italy, either by sea or land. Not that I have any great hopes of that, for, I think, there is a core of disease in me not easy to pull out... If I should die... [blanked out] I shall be obliged to set off in less than a month. Do not, dear Brown, tease yourself about me. You must fill up your time as well as you can, and as happily. You must think of my faults as lightly as you can. When I have health I will bring up the long arrears of letters I owe you... My

book has had good success among the literary people, and I believe a moderate sale.

I have seen very few people that we know. Haslam has visited me more than anyone. I would go to Dilke and make some enquiries after you, if I could with any bearable sensation; [here again the names have been blanked from the copy letter, and the ones put in are supersession] but a person I am not quite used to causes an oppression on my chest. [Keats had fallen out with Mrs Hunt over an opened letter.] Last week I received a letter from Shelley at Pisa, of a very kind nature, asking me to pass the winter with him.

Hunt has behaved very kindly to me. You shall hear again from me shortly.

Your affectionate friend,
John Keats

Keats wrote again to Brown, in some desperation, towards the end of August:

My Dear Brown,

I ought to be off at the end of this week, as the cold winds begin to blow towards evening; but I will wait till I have your answer to this. I am to be introduced, before I set out, to a Dr Clark, a Physician settled at Rome, who promises to befriend me in every way there. The sale of my book is very slow, though it has been very highly rated. One of the causes, I understand from different quarters, of the unpopularity of this new book, and the others also, is the offence the ladies take at me. On thinking that matter over, I am certain that I have said nothing in a spirit to displease any woman I would care to please; but still there is a tendency to class women in my books with roses and sweetmeats, – they never see themselves dominant. If ever I come to publish 'Lucy Vaughan Lloyd' there will be some picking for squeamish stomachs. I will say no more, but, waiting in anxiety for your answer, doff my hat, and make a purse as long as I can.

Your affectionate friend
John Keats

It seems that even at this late stage Keats still hoped that Charles Brown would accompany him to Italy.

The next letter was written aboard the *Maria Crowther* which sailed from Portsmouth on the 29th of September. See Part 3 (The Joseph Severn story) for letters from the *Maria Crowther*, Naples and Rome Italy.

As the news of Keats filtered through from Italy within Severn's letters, raising and then deflating the hopes of his friends waiting in England, they feared the worst. Throughout February Brown felt a tension within his breast. His breathing became laboured, he described his chest clamped with bands of steel. He realised that Keats would not recover and prayed for his friend's suffering to end. But when Severn's letter arrived in Early March, his hands trembled as he broke the seal. As his blurred eyes tried to take in its contents the full horror of the situation struck him dumb.

On the 18th of March, Brown wrote to John Taylor, Keats' publisher:

"It is all over. I leave to you the care of inserting his death in the papers, – word it as you please, – you will do it better than I can, – in fact I cant do it."

Fanny Brawne, distraught, cut her long hair short, dressed in black she wandered about the heath. A white-faced Brown mourned deeply for his dearest friend. He wrote to Joseph Severn and mentioned Fanny Brawne.

"It is now five days since she heard it. I shall not speak of the first shock, nor of the following days, it is enough she is now pretty well and thro'out she has shown a firmness of mind which I little expected from one so young, and under such a load of grief."

On the 27th of March Fanny Brawne put her pen to paper and expressed her grief to Keats' sister.

Tuesday Afternoon March 27, 1821

You will forgive me, I am sure, my dear Fanny, that I did not write to you before. I could not for my own sake and I would not for yours, as it was better you should be prepared for what, even knowing as much as you did, you could not expect. I should like to hear that you my dearest Sister are well, for myself, I am patient resigned, very resigned. I know my Keats is happy, happier a thousand times than he could have been here, for Fanny, you do not, you never can know how much he has suffered. So much that I do believe, were it in my power I would not bring him back. All that grieves me now is that I was not with him, and so near it as I was. Some day my dear girl I will tell you the reason and give you additional cause to hate those who should have been his friends, and yet it was a great deal through his kindness for me for he foresaw what would happen, he at least was never deceived about his complaint, though the Doctors were ignorant and unfeeling enough to send him to that wretched country to die, for it is now known that his recovery was impossible before he left us, and he might have died here with so many friends to soothe him and me, me with him. All we have to console ourselves with is the great joy he felt that all his misfortunes were at an end. At the very last he said 'I am dying thank god the time is come', and in a letter from Mr Severn written about a fortnight before he died and which was not shown to me, so that I thought he would live months at least, if he did not recover, he says 'he is still alive and calm, if I say more it will be too much, yet at times I have thought him better but he would not hear of it, the

61

thought of recovery is beyond every thing dreadful to him – we dare not perceive any improvement for the hope of death seems his only comfort, he talks of the quiet grave as the first rest he can ever have.' In that letter he mentions that he had given directions how he would be buried, the purse you sent him and your last letter (which he never read, for he would never open either your letters or mine after he left England) with some hair, I believe mine, he desired to be placed in his coffin. The truth is I cannot very well go on at present with this, another time I will tell you more, what I wish to say now relates to yourself, my Mother is coming to see you soon. If you are in Pancrass lane she will call next Friday, that is if it be not disagreeable to Mr Abbey. [Brown wrote to Severn on the 23 March: 'I wrote to Haslam to call on Abbey, and if Abbey will permit it, Mrs Brawne and Mrs Dilke will call on Miss Keats. They are in mourning next door' – Richard Abbey, the Keats' siblings' guardian was very restrictive, he had refused Fanny permission to visit her brother or he her.]

Do you think he would allow you to stay with us a short time? I have desired my Mother to ask him, though I do not know how shc will prevail on herself to do it, for she is afraid of him, but Mrs Dilke will be with her to give her courage. And now my dear I must hope you will favour me with your company, it will I assure you be a real favour. And yet I hardly like to press you to make such a dull visit. I once hoped for a very different one from you, I used to anticipate the pleasure I should feel in showing every kindness and attention in my power to you. And I felt so happy when he desired me to write to you while he was away. I little thought how it would turn out. I have just recollected that perhaps you will not wish to come out so soon. Fix your own time my dear, only come. Will you have the kindness to write to me, by return of post, if you can, to say if Friday will be too soon for you to see my Mother, and if you will come, and when. I ask you with more confidence though there is little or nothing to amuse us, because I have heard you lead a very dull life in Abbey's family – but we will do as much as we can to amuse you and to prevent your thinking of any thing to make you unhappy. You must consider my Mother as more than a stranger for your brother loved her very much, and used often to wish she could go with him, and had he returned I should have been his wife and he would have lived with us. [Here Fanny Brawne confirms her engagement to Keats and her plans as his future wife.] All, all now in vain – could we have foreseen – but he did foresee and everyone thought it was only his habit of looking for the worst. Though you are the only person in the world I wish to see, I will own I do not expect it. Your Guardian is said to be much more than strict, and was so particular in refusing to let your brothers take you out, that I have not the least hope, but as much as we can do shall, with your consent, be tried and if it is in vain I will, before you leave London, call on you – If Mr Abbey should so far think of it to ask who we are, you may if you like say my Mother is a widow and has two children besides me, both very young – send me an answer as soon as you can conveniently – My Mother desires her love to you and I send a thousand good wishes to my dear sister God bless her.

Frances Brawne

What the Brawnes hadn't realised was that the Abbeys opened and read letters addressed to their ward before passing them to her – therefore derogatory remarks made about the way they behaved only made matters worse.

Barely two weeks had passed after the news of Keats' death when Taylor & Hessey, Keats' publishers, began to collect material for a biography. John Taylor was genuinely concerned with promoting Keats' fame, and would have likely produced a competent work. Brown, however, was furious at what he termed this indecent haste. He told Taylor that it looked as if his friends had been collecting information about his life in expectation of his death, and this was likely to have been so. Joseph Severn sent brown all the letters and other papers that he had in Rome. Excepting those he had placed within the coffin. Brown refused to give Taylor any information. Saying in a letter to Severn, "I will not consent to be a party in a bookseller's job. I rejoice you sent me the papers, and under the circumstances I think you will rejoice likewise." John Taylor's feelings toward Brown changed from then on, and Brown mistrusted Taylor.

The friends began to fall out with each other, the magic of their poet had for the time being evaporated. However Severn and Brown began a close relationship. Severn said, "Brown, if anyone is to write anything about him it must be you."

Brown and Severn put their ideas forward for a Keats memorial in Italy. Severn had already designed a monument; a Grecian altar with a half strung Lyre engraved upon it.

Brown believed that Keats' friends should have the chance of composing the epitaph. When nothing came of it, Brown decided to put forward something of his own, and wrote for the others approval:

THIS GRAVE CONTAINS ALL THAT WAS MORTAL OF A YOUNG ENGLISH POET, WHO ON HIS DEATH-BED, IN BITTER ANGUISH AT THE NEGLECT OF HIS COUNTRYMEN, DESIRED THESE WORDS TO BE ENGRAVEN ON HIS TOMB-STONE. "HERE LIES ONE WHOSE NAME WAS WRIT IN WATER."

Keats had told Brown almost jokingly that this inscription was his wish should he die. Brown recognised it as a phrase from *Henry VIII*. This then was a remembrance of

Shakespeare whom Keats would have chosen above all to sum up his life. Leigh Hunt, Charles Dilke, and other friends shown the proposed inscription approved. And the words slightly altered appear on the poet's tomb.

Brown took on the task of executor to the poet's will. He called on Richard Abbey to ascertain the extent of the poet's estate, and bills unpaid. He divided Keats' books amongst his friends, as he had been instructed, keeping Bacon's *Advancement of Learning* which Keats had owned as a boy in memory. He also took back *The Anatomy of Learning* which he himself had given. The volumes of Beaumont and Fletcher that Keats and he had read with pleasure two years before, during Keats' first spring at Wentworth Place were also consigned to his bundle. George Keats, disappointed, received nothing.

Hampstead had now a coldness about it, all the literary magic was gone. New people moved into the properties vacated by Brown's circle. He felt lonely and dispirited and began to think of going abroad. The idea of living in Italy was still in his mind. He had recently seen Leigh Hunt and his family excitedly boarding a coach at the beginning of their own Italian adventure. His relationship with Abigail was difficult, she threatened to move out of Wentworth Place and take the boy Carlino off to Ireland. His affection for Abigail had waned, however he took his responsibility as the boy's father seriously, and he doted on Carlino. At the beginning of 1822 the problem worsened, but then Abigail had a change of heart and handed the boy over to his father. Maria Dilke said she would take care of the child. Thomas Richards, Clerk of Ordnance at the Tower and an ex-Clarke's Schoolboy offered to bring up the boy with his own children. Brown thought that it might be good for Carlino to live within a family. As March came to an end he was still undecided. Finally his mind was made up, it was possible that the strong-minded Abigail might try to gain legal custody.

Brown decided to take Carlino out of the country, they would go together to Italy.

With the Dilke family moved to Westminster and Brown wanting to begin his travels, the two joint owners of Wentworth Place decided to lease out the property and advertised for a leaseholder. However by that November the house had not been taken. It looked as if Brown would be kept in England for a few more months. Then old Mr Dilke of Chichester offered him a way out, he agreed to take over Brown's half of the house. The assignment was sealed in scarlet wax with a Tassie head of Shakespeare, a final gesture that would have pleased Keats had he been watching.

Brown with his infant son set out for Italy. By August the 31st they had reached Pisa. An old acquaintance waited for them, Leigh Hunt. Hunt then introduced him to Lord Byron. Brown had little time for the dissolute poet who had so cruelly criticised Keats' work. But on hearing that on Keats' death Byron had ordered all his derogatory comments removed from his work, Brown's opinion softened. "And foolish soul that I am this quite satisfied me," he wrote. After this Brown was left alone when the Hunts and Byron moved to Genoa. Brown revelled in the Italian lifestyle, he wrote in a letter to Richards, "I am more a citizen of the world than an Englishman." And yet England and his English friends remained in his thoughts, and there was one of whom he was constantly reminded.

Severn was fretting over the gravestone for Keats. He disliked Brown's suggested inscription and proposed yet another. Two years had passed since Keats' death and the stone was still not in place. Severn asked Brown to consider a memorial in England. Brown was steadfast still in supporting the poet, yet he knew that the English press still scoffed at Keats' work. He replied to Severn, "His fame is not sufficiently general and a monument to his memory might even retard it, it might provoke ill nature, (shall I say ridicule). In prudence we ought to wait awhile, ten years hence to my mind, is time enough."

And so the friendly arguments continued. Severn refused contributions from others wanting to subscribe toward the Italian memorial. He was even unwilling to accept Brown's payment until he demanded his rights; saying, "You must not have all the pleasure of this." By June 1823 Brown was in Florence, leaving Carlino with an Italian family at Pisa. He went with a beneficial heart to stay with Severn. Severn, who now considered Brown his closest friend delighted him by passing to him the business of running his household, and under his dedicated management he produced an ordered house. A month later Carlino came on a visit, and in one of his miniature portraits Severn captured a blue-eyed, fair-haired child whose features had, Severn thought, "a remarkable likeness to his mother's."

Byron, preparing to leave to fight for 'the poor Greeks' arrived with Edward Trelawny. Severn painted two small portraits for them. Byron was delighted. Brown declared that he had never seen portraits done with such skill and speed. Byron left Italy for Greece. Brown and Severn began a two-month sightseeing tour. In October they returned to Florence to find the Hunts with yet another child, and complaining bitterly about Byron. Byron had encouraged Leigh Hunt in his Italian adventure, given some financial assistance and the copyright of his 'Vision of Judgement' for Hunt's new *Liberal Magazine*. He had then ridiculed the publication, and after this had been rude to Marianne, confirming his dislike for her and the Hunt children. Byron then left the Hunts for the war in Greece without a word of farewell. When Brown had listened to Hunt's account of this behaviour what regard he may have had for Byron evaporated.

A few months later when the news of Byron's death from fever in the marshes of Missolonghi became known, Brown pronounced a harsh judgement on the poet. "Talk of Byron as a poet 'ad libitum' but as a man you had better be silent."

After a few days at Florence, Severn and Brown travelled to Rome. Together they went to the cemetery where Keats was interred in the place for non-Catholics, outside of the Aurelian Wall. He gazed from a distance at the Pyramid tomb of Caius Cestius but felt no emotion. "A grave never affects me, the living man was a stranger to it, and it contains only a clod like itself." Passing through the city he had descended the Spanish Steps, walked along the Piazza-Di-Spagna, by the reddish coloured apartment building, and under the window of the room where Keats had breathed his last. The square and buildings bathed in bright sunlight seemed a more fitting memorial to his friend than the lonely cemetery. "I have taught myself to think with pleasure of his having been alive and been my friend, and not with sorrow at his death. If your eternal sorrowers think it very odd in me – why, – I'm an odd fellow you know, and so let the argument end."

At Florence, Leigh Hunt stared financial ruin in the face; his business affairs were in disarray. Marianne with another baby at her bosom adding to the large family already a drain on dwindling funds. "Will Hunt never have done?" cried Brown. And now Hunt's brother John in England demanded settlement of a supposed £2,000 debt. Hunt turned to Brown for help. Brown set his accountant's mind to work in an effort to save the day. How this was accomplished is of no importance here. However the astute set of accounts he prepared were agreed upon. Sick and depressed Hunt wanted to return to England. On their last night in Italy a small farewell party at the Villa-Morandi was attended by Brown and Severn. The next morning the Hunts took leave of The Valley of Ladies. Leigh Hunt said, "The grave face of Brown was not so easily to be parted with, I was obliged to gulp down a sensation in the throat, such as men cannot very well afford to confess."

By the autumn of that year Brown had other things on his mind. He had become attracted to a widow lady of about his own age. He said, "I woke in the middle of last night, and could not go to sleep again for thinking of my dear Euphemia. To be caught at last! is it not an uncommonly foolish – sensible sort of thing? she has most beautiful eyes, forehead, nose, mouth, chin, cheeks, neck and all that, and such a figure, such a shape. She wants me to marry her! I've made her a very handsome offer, – to be a governess to the boy, or my housekeeper, – whichever she likes best, and if neither of these pleases, why I must be her 'amico' in a private way, for I'll have nothing to do with priests!"

Charles Brown was still a married man and had his principles. The lady had principles of her own and would not accept his offer and soon disappeared from the scene. Brown now became anxious about money, he was living beyond his means, and payment for his articles did not materialise. He had a wide circle of friends and entertained lavishly, Carlino was living with him but he was duty bound to send Abigail an allowance. And now he moved into a new larger house in Florence. As he worried, news came that raised his spirits. His lifetime friend Charles Dilke, who he hadn't seen for four years was coming to Italy, and would arrive at Florence in September. In the meantime he continued entertaining his friends, they ate his food, drank his wine and reduced his wealth! Walter Savage Landor (poet and writer) walked in one day, asking Brown if he knew of a portrait of Shelley. Brown wrote to Marianne Hunt, asking her to enquire of Mary Shelley. Marianne herself had cut several silhouettes of the poet, and these she sent off to Italy. (There is no record of these being received, and maybe they were lost in transit). Brown was now sleeping in the bed that had belonged to Shelley, and employed Maddalena, who had been Shelley's servant in Florence. Shelley was not forgotten. Brown for the first time since his arrival in Italy began to feel unwell. He began to diet, gave up wine drinking only water. Took up regular exercise, going on long walks around Florence. Dilke arrived, answering the doorbell, Maddalena found a portly Englishman who had a bearing of authority and looked older than his 36 years. He said good day, entered and stood warming himself by the stove. The two old friends met with smiles and friendly handshakes. Brown described Dilke as "a grave, stout, comely old gentleman." Dilke in return thought Brown looked young and fit, the Italian life seemed to agree with him. In fact Brown was the elder of the two, being only a few months away from his fortieth birthday.

The best china was brought out, and Brown abandoned his diet. Dilke was accompanied by his only son Charley, now sixteen years old and finished with his schooling in the City of Westminster. Charley would stay over in Italy with Brown to broaden his education. Together they went on a visit to the Landors. Brown compared the two men, and noted that they seemed to take a liking for each other. Dilke, a keen student of Greek history had found a kindred spirit. Brown wrote little of their visit to Rome, except to say that he had chosen to stay with Severn, rather than at the Inn with the Dilkes. It was Dilke who recorded their visit to Keats' grave. "Our group approached the grave in silence, the grave now marked with a stone as yet unweathered, as Charley began to weep I could hardly conceal my emotion, Brown turned away to hide his own grief." They continued on their travels to Naples, to Mola-di-Gaeta, where Brown read Spenser under the orange trees in memory of Keats. On their return to Florence Dilke said good-bye to his only son and took a ship back to England.

Charley was to stay with Brown for two years until he went up to Cambridge. Brown heard from Leigh Hunt in England that he was working on a new book. It was to be his recollections of poets and writers that he had known. He intimated that both Brown and Keats would be included within the pages. Brown proposed a partnership in the work. "This of course supposes me in England with fifty other suppositions; Dreaming is mightily pleasant." However he secretly wished that Hunt wouldn't do it. Charley Dilke left for England the following summer after only a year in Italy suffering from homesickness.

And now Brown's life became disturbed by another distraction; Lady King, a fine looking woman of about his own age, and of independent means. She wanted to move in with him, and as she said, "Take up joint housekeeping." Brown was tempted and discussed her proposal with Carlino. With his practical mind the boy pointed out the advantages of an extra income. Brown however doubted that such an arrangement would remain platonic. Carlino suggested marriage, to which his father replied, "you forget I already have a wife." During that summer Brown commissioned the sculptor Andrew Wilson, a friend of Joseph Severn's to make a head and shoulders bust of himself. In that same year Brown moved house once again, to number 1905 Via Maggia, and at this address Joseph Severn married Elizabeth Montgomerie. After their marriage the couple set up house in Rome.

Then there arrived at Via Maggia the adventurer Trelawny, the companion of Lord Byron in the Greek tragedy. Trelawny returned from the Greek wars low in spirits and funds, and Brown invited him into his home. Trelawny, a friend of Shelley, had attended the poet's cremation and on impulse had thrust his hand into the fire to retrieve the heart. His hand burnt still bore the scars. Brown encouraged Trelawny to write his autobiography. He announced, "I am required to write my life history, Brown and Landor urge me on, seventy pages are already done." Trelawny's literary prowess was not up to that of his friends and most of his work had to be rewritten. In March 1829 he was still living at Via Maggia and planning to write about Shelley's life. And then two more visitors arrived; James Cobbett and his sister, the children of William Cobbett. (William Cobbett – 1763–1835, writer and politician, famous for his *History of Protestant Reformation* and *Rural Rides*.) The Cobbetts left for Rome with a paper by Brown on housekeeping in Italy.

71

As the 1820s came to a close, Brown received a reminder of Keats. A letter from the French publisher 'Galignani' arrived from Paris, they were searching for any unpublished Keats poems. They would go into print if enough material came to light. Brown replied, mentioning the unpublished manuscripts and letters in his possession.

In December 1829, eight years after the poet's death, he wrote three begging letters, one to Fanny Brawne whom he had neglected since his move to Italy. Would she allow him to use poems and letters which had concerned her? Another letter recipient, Joseph Severn answered, "I can supply ample material, I shall be proud to make my appearance as an unchanged friend of John Keats." Brown had written in all ignorance of Fanny's circumstances. She received what must have seemed a somewhat harassing letter within a week of her mother's funeral, after her horrific death at the door of Wentworth Place. On the 26 November, the night was dark and windy, Mrs Brawne, Fanny's mother, was showing a guest to the door when a gust of wind directed the flame of the candle she was carrying on to the ruff of her sleeve. The flame quickly spread to the front of her dress, and before she could receive help she was badly burned. Mrs Brawne was buried at St Martin-in-the-Fields on the 1st of that December.

Miss Brawne, Wentworth Place, Hampstead.

Florence, 17th December

My dear Miss Brawne,

Without any apology for our long silence, let me hope you are in the best of health, that your mother is better, and that Margaret is never ailing; to which I add a merry Xmas and a happy new year to all. Now, with these good wishes, I may begin. A few days ago, I received a letter from the Galignani in Paris telling me they are on the eve of publishing the works of Keats, and asking for his autograph. I sent it to them, with a letter stating it was always my intention to write his life, and annex it to a Tragedy of his, together with some unpublished poems in my possession, whenever his countrymen should have learnt to value his poetry. I also told them I believed that time was arrived, as needs it must, sooner or later; but that I was fearful it was too late for me to enter into any arrangement with them. Whatever their answer may be, I am resolved to write his life, persuaded that no one, except yourself knew him better. Leigh Hunt's account of him is worse than disappointing. [Leigh Hunt's *Lord Byron and Some of His Contemporaries* – 1828, in which Hunt had depicted Keats as a weakling] I cannot bear it; seems as if Hunt was so impressed by his illness, that he had utterly forgotten him in health. This is a dreadful mistake, because it is our duty to his memory to show the ruin his enemies had affected; and I will not spare them.

It is not my present purpose to enter into any criticism on his works, but let it be simply a biography; and, to make that as vivid as possible, I shall incorporate into it passages from letters to me, and to his brothers, – which last are in my possession; together with passages from particular poems, or entire ones, relating to himself, always avoiding those which regard you, unless you let me know that I may, without mentioning your name, introduce them. There are, however, two of his letters which I wish to give entire; one written when he despaired of Tom's recovery, the other when he despaired of his own. This latter one is of the most painful description; therefore I wish it to be known, that Gifford and Lockhart may be thoroughly hated and despised. [The columnists who were responsible for the attacks upon Keats and Leigh Hunt in the *Edinburgh Magazine*.]

The question is whether you will object to it; I think you will not. Though much of it regards you, your name is never once mentioned. Then again, those poems addressed to you, which you permitted me to

73

copy, – may I publish them? It is impossible for me to judge of your feelings on the subject; but whatever they are, you are certain that I shall obey them. To my mind you ought to consent, as no greater honour can be paid to a woman than to be beloved by such a man as Keats. I am aware that, at a more recent period, you would have been startled at its being alluded to; but consider that eight years have passed away; and now, no one, if you do not, can object to it. Besides, Hunt has alluded to you, and what more will it be to give his poems addressed to that lady? Your name will still remain as secret to the world as before. I shall of course scrupulously avoid intimating who you are, or in what part of England you reside. As his love for you formed so great a part of him, we may be doing him an injustice in being silent on it: Indeed something must be said especially as Hunt has said something. We live among strange customs; for had you been husband and wife, though but for an hour, everyone would have thought himself at liberty publicly to speak of, and all about you; but as you were only so in your hearts, it seems, as it were, improper. Think of it in your best train for thinking, my dear Miss Brawne, and let me know your decision. I have turned it in my mind a great deal, and find nothing to confess the truth freely, – against it. Three months ago I heard you were at Bruges, on a visit to your aunt; but I suppose you are, by this time returned.

Give my kindest remembrances to Mrs Brawne and Margaret. [As said, Browne had no knowledge of Mrs Brawne's so recent death.] Carlino and I lead very comfortable, happy, and healthy lives, with short lessons, long walks, and now and then, a game at romps, or "ballo grande" at the Opera.

Believe me always.
Yours most sincerely,
Cha's Brown

This letter must have seemed to Fanny a most strange and weedling correspondence, however that she sat down to answer it almost at once shows a depth of character beyond what could have been expected in her disturbed circumstance, having buried her mother just three weeks before.

The letter that we have has been termed a draft copy; certainly it is full of mistakes and crossings-out. No attempt to replicate these errors and crossings-out has been made here, the gist of the letter has been assembled in the best way possible.

29 December 1829, Hampstead

My dear Mr Brown,

As the aggressor I am too happy to escape the apologies I owe you on my long silence, not gladly to take your hint and say nothing about it, the best reparation I can make is to answer your letter of today as soon as possible, although I received it only this morning; in the hours that have intervened before I sat down to answer it, my feelings have entirely changed on the subject of the request it contains. Perhaps you will think I was opposed to it, and am now come over to your side of the question, but it is just the contrary. had I answered your letter immediately I should have told you that I considered myself so entirely unconnected with Mr Keats, except for my own feelings, that nothing published respecting him could affect me, but now I see it differently. We have all our little world in which we figure and I cannot help expressing some disinclination that the few acquaintances I have should be able to obtain such a key to my sensations. Having said so much you will probably conclude that I mean to refuse our request. Perhaps when I assure you that though my opinion has changed, my intention of complying in every respect with your wishes remains, you will think I am mentioning my objections to make favour of my consent, but indeed my dear Mr Brown if you do, you mistake me entirely. It is only to justify myself I own, that I state all I think to you. I am very grateful, nor ought I have gone so far without thanking you for your kindness and consideration in writing to me on the subject. I assure you I should not have hinted that your wishes were painful to me did I not feel the suffering myself to be even alluded to was a want of pride. So far am I from possessing overstrained delicacy, that the circumstance of its being a mere love story is the least of my concern; on the contrary, had I been his wife I should have felt my present reluctance would have been so much stronger that I think I must have made it my request that you would relinquish your intention. The only thing that saves me now, is that so few can know I am in any way implicated, and that of those few, I may hope the greater number may never see the book in Question.

Do then entirely as you please, and be assured that I comply with your wishes, rather because they are yours, than with the expectation of any good that can be done. I fear the kindest act would be to let him rest for ever in the obscurity to which unhappy circumstance have condemned him. [Fanny cannot have known just how wrong she was in making this statement.] Will the writings that remain of his rescue him from it? You can tell better than I, and are more impartial on the subject, my wish has long been that his name, his very name could be forgotten by every one but myself, that I have often wished most intensely.

To your publishing his poems addressed to me, I do not see there can be any objection after the subject has been alluded to, if you think them worthy of him.

I entirely agree with you that if his life is to be published no part ought to be kept back, for all you can show is his character, his life was too short and too unfortunate for any thing else. I have no doubt that his talents would have been great, not the less for their being developed rather late which I believe was the case; all I fear is whether he has left enough to make people believe that. If I could think so, I should consider it right to make that sacrifice to his reputation that I now do to your kind motives. Not that even the establishment of his fame would give me the pleasure it ought. Without claiming to much constancy for myself I may truly say that he is well remembered by me, and that satisfied with that I could wish no one but myself knew he ever existed, but I confess as he was so much calumniated and suffered so much from it, it is perhaps the duty of those who loved him to vindicate him also, and if it can be done, all the friends that time has left him, and I above all must be deeply indebted to you. I am glad you feel that Mr Hunt gave him a weakness of character that surely only belonged to his ill health. Mr Hazlitt, if I remember rightly in his remarks used five or six years ago is still more positive in fixing it on him. I should be glad if you could disprove I was a very poor judge of character ten years ago, and probably overrated every good quality he had, but surely they go too far on the other side; after all he was but four and twenty when his illness began and he had gone through a great deal of vexation before.

Here this remarkable letter ends. There is no signature, so it is possible that some small part is missing. The letter was addressed to 'Signor Charles Brown. Gentiluomo Inglesi. Firenze. Italia'. Although giving Brown freedom to publish at will, she seems to have certainly put him firmly in place!

In a letter to the poet's sister, Francis 'Fanny' Keats, dated the 18 September 1820, after Keats had left Hampstead for Italy; Fanny Brawne wrote about Keats' numerous friends.

"I am certain he has some spell that attaches them to him, or else he has fortunately met with a set of friends that I did not believe could be found in the world."

Brown's letter to Charles Wentworth Dilke brought up the thorny subject of Keats' financial problems during the year before his death. Brown had accused John's brother George of being in part responsible. George had written to Dilke in 1824 looking for his support against the accusations coming from England. Dilke sent Brown in Italy a copy of the letter together with a summary of how he saw the transactions between the brothers, and that he would vindicate George. Brown answered; "no one would rejoice more than myself to find him guiltless of the charge against him." During a search through a bundle of Keats' old papers and letters in preparation for the planned life story, he came across something which seemed to prove his side of the argument. Brown wrote again to Joseph Severn, "After a while, as if by an invisible hand, a passage in one of George's own letters was turned towards me, the writing there gave a lie direct to the groundwork of his defence. I then searched further, and found an account of Abbey's. With these two documents I was instantly enabled to prove that every title of his defence was false." Dilke became enraged! Years before Keats had said, "Dilke has no character unless he has made up his mind about everything." He had decided that George was innocent, now confronted with Brown's evidence he still refused to believe in George's guilt. He took the account before him as an attack on his integrity. He answered Brown's letter in unrestrained anger, with such insolence that as he read the blood drained from Brown's face. He replied on the 31st of March 1830; "My dear Dilke, You have wounded me to the quick. I could not have believed that anyone I am acquainted with, far less you, would treat me both in matter and manner with such injustice. There are some things said, that when said can never be undone." Dilke, by that one letter had ended a friendship which had lasted from their schooldays.

Brown buried himself in work, collecting and collating the letters and works of Keats. He wrote to Leigh Hunt asking for Charles Cowden Clarke's address. "Can Clarke tell me in what parish Keats was born in, and anything he may know of his schooldays?" He also started work on something that he had wished to do for several years, preparing to write a book on Shakespeare. People still came on visits, for the most part men with literary interests. Crabb Robinson the diarist stayed a while, read Brown's manuscript on Shakespeare, and despite being asked not to comment on the unfinished work he then went on to visit Landor where he openly discussed what he had seen. Landor, Brown said, wrote to Leigh Hunt; "That no man ever had an understanding of Shakespeare like myself [Brown]. True or not, this is the greatest compliment that I have ever received."

In 1930, Edward Trelawny, whose literary skill had improved with the help of Brown, completed his autobiography. This gave Brown a chance to forward Keats' fame. He offered Trelawny a collection of quotations to use as chapter headings. And Trelawny was the first to make use of *Otho the Great and King Stephen*. Mary Shelley edited the book, and in 1831 it was published anonymously. As agreed Brown received a share of the profits.

Carlino was taken out of school to be tutored by his father. And some of Brown's friends accused the doting father of allowing the boy to run wild. Brown was considering returning to England where Carlino might finish his education.

In 1832 another Keats' supporter, one of the first collectors of the poet's work, Richard Woodhouse arrived on Brown's doorstep. Woodhouse, the slight red-headed lawyer, hardly taller than Keats himself, had arrived in Italy, seeking, as so many before him, a cure for his tuberculosis. Like Keats his journey was in vain, for just a few months later he returned to England to die in his early forties. Woodhouse had recognised Keats' genius at the very beginning of their acquaintance. He had given himself the task of copying any of the poet's work that came his way. Brown began to reveal more poems and letters. Woodhouse had commissioned copies of the Severn miniature of Keats, and now made a present of one to a delighted Brown who thought the plaster medallion "quite a small piece of magic". Years before, at a card party on the 19th of April 1818, Brown had conceived what Keats had called, "one of his funny odd dislikes" for Woodhouse. But now with their latest meeting this 'odd dislike' soon disappeared. And when a few weeks later Woodhouse left him, he told Severn that he had come to like the lawyer very much. He also said, "Woodhouse thinks that one or two of the quotations in Trelawny's book will be of great service to the fame of Keats, and has made me promise to write the life of our dear friend in my quiet country nook during this winter."

In the summer of 1833 Richard Monckton Milnes arrived in Italy. A young man just down from Cambridge, where he had been the leader of a student group who were endeavouring to promote Keats' poetry and bring it to the public's notice. At their own expense they had reprinted Shelley's 'Adonais'.

Whilst on his 'Grand Tour', Milnes had been taken ill and it was fortunate for him that he happened to be in Florence, where Landor had taken him in at the Villa Gherardesca. Charles Brown visiting Landor found the 24-year-old academic convalescing in the garden. They fell into easy conversation; Milnes had been to Rome, visited the cemetery and the graves of Keats and Shelley, and had learned from Severn all that the painter could tell. Now it became Brown's turn to pour out his heart. Milnes listened intently, hardly containing his excitement, and was astounded when Brown told of the amount of unpublished work that still existed. By so doing he, without knowing it, planted the seeds for the first Keats' biography.

Brown's health began to fade, he picked up his diet again and the long walks about Florence. One day in the Vieusseux's library he suffered an apoplectic fit, and from then on never fully regained his health. He said, "this illness has left me with a hell of nervousness." Later that same year he left Italy to return to his own country. In the summer of 1835 he retired, moving into a cottage situated at Laira Green in the quiet countryside two miles from Plymouth. The people of his neighbourhood were not of a literary set. He said, "some of my neighbours are rather dull and sickly, and Tories into the bargain." Brown soon found himself taken up with the Plymouth Institute where he gave his lectures on the Shakespeare Sonnets. A talk he gave on 'The Intellectual History of Florence' was well received with applause and compliments from the assembly, and he soon found himself offered the post of Curator of the Library. In the evening of December the 29th 1836, in the large hall of the Plymouth Athenaeum, Charles Brown gave the very first public lecture on the poet Keats. The hall was full to its capacity with dignitaries and men of trade from the town, none of whom had read any of Keats' poems. For three hours he spoke on the poet's life and works, he spoke of Keats as his friend, and at times found his throat restricted by emotion. When he spoke out against *The Quarterly* which was a Tory publication, telling how he believed they had helped to destroy Keats, some of the audience resented the implications. But they accepted him as one of superior knowledge amongst those who were ignorant on the subject.

He continued to work on his Shakespeare, and in 1838, Bohn of King William Street published *Shakespeare's Autobiographical Poems* by Charles Armitage-Brown. Brown began to use his brother's Christian name 'Armitage' with a hyphen, brought about because Trelawny had teased him that Brown was a common tribal name! The book for the most part received good reviews, with one notable exception – Dilke. In the 'Athenaeum' he strongly criticised his friend of thirty years. This was the last nail in the coffin driven home, ending the Brown–Dilke friendship for ever.

Brown missed the life in Italy and the stream of intellectual visitors to his home. However Walter Savage Landor arrived at Laira Cottage to renew their acquaintance (Landor – 1775–1864 author of note). He had the look of a prophet, features of a superior being. Charles Armitage-Brown was envious, and said, "all the women in Plymouth fell in love with him." When Landor left, Brown's loneliness deepened. His son Carlino was away in London studying for a profession in engineering. And as his health weakened, he wrote, "I have a house and yet can boast no home." He placed an advert in the local paper for a lodger. '*The advertiser seeks a companion, by no means a boarder and lodger for profit.*' Now his lectures at the Plymouth Institute had lost their popularity, articles that he wrote for local newspapers were being returned. The Tories of the Plymouth Institute, controlling local commerce, were closing ranks, turning against the dyed-in-the-wool Liberal. Carlino wrote to his father, asking him to use his influence with his friend, Richard Monckton Milnes, now an MP. Brown replied, "You could have hardly pitched on any MP less likely to forward your interests than Mr Milnes; I have no claim on him whatever, and he is an absolute Tory."

Brown's financial difficulties increased, a tenant had fled, owing a large amount in unpaid rents. He had paid for the printing of his Shakespeare Biography, and although it was selling, his publisher had not paid any of the royalties due. Carlino had discussed his father's troubles with May, the proprietor of *The Plymouth and Devonport Weekly Journal*. May had withheld payment for articles, and refused to accept further contributions which he said might offend churchmen and elders. Brown no longer wrote for the *Journal*, and sent the rejected articles to the *Devonport Independent*, whose editor obliged, printing Brown's 'The Church in Danger' and a ballad entitled 'The Tory's Confession'.

Brown now 53 found another lady, however he soon discovered that her designs were different to his own, she wished for marriage. Her name was Jane Renfry, a desperate spinster. Brown told Carlino, "she says that she is in love with me." Elizabeth the housekeeper called her Crazy Jane. Brown said, "she weeps at my indifference! I am lonely," he told Carlino, "but she would make me as crazy as herself and you are aware that I am still another's husband, be it in name only."

In 1840, Richard Monckton Milnes came across Brown's diary of his tours of Scotland, published in the *London Journal*, and wrote to him asking if there were any works of Keats that the friend of the poet would release for publication. Brown now realising that he would never be able to do so himself, offered Monkton Milnes the task of establishing Keats' fame by writing what was to be the first biography. Brown could not have made a better choice. Leigh Hunt in his recollections had portrayed Keats as a weakling, stricken with consumption.

Joseph Severn was not up to it, for as Brown told him "the task would be to great for such an inadequate writer." In Brown's eyes John Taylor, Keats' publisher, had disqualified himself by becoming, as Brown termed him a 'Book Seller' and one who had refused to publish a second edition of Keats' poems, or give up the copyright that he held on them. He also considered unworthy, Dilke and Keats' brother George.

Brown felt it was time to make changes to his life. He decided to let Carlino go to New Zealand, and to follow on himself when the last of his business in England had been finalised. The cottage at Laira Green was put up for sale. '*A freehold cottage, being No: 2, Laira Green. Near Plymouth. Now in the occupation of Charles Brown esq. With two Parlours, two Kitchens, five Bedrooms, a Pantry, China closet and other offices, with pleasant gardens and a Greenhouse etc.*' (The cottage sold for the sum of £225.)

Almost twenty years after Keats' death, Charles Armitage-Brown, nervous and unwell, began the task of revising his life of the poet. In the revision he did not incriminate George; Keats' brother was spared. The dastardly business of Blackwood's and the *Quarterly*, with a chapter on Keats' illness were added. Brown wrote to Monckton Milnes. "I am ready to repose in you, will you undertake the task?" Milnes eagerly accepted by return. (Richard Monckton Milnes – Later 1st baron Lord Houghton.)

Brown went with Carlino on a last visit to London and Hampstead, where they saw the building extension at Wentworth Place. Brown carried with him the parcel of papers containing all Keats' unpublished works and letters in his possession. That same day the valuable package went by coach to Monckton Milnes. Brown retained a few personal souvenirs to take with him to New Zealand.

Early in 1841 Carlino emigrated. Before his own departure Brown wrote, "I shall wish myself many happy returns of the day in New Zealand." He would be 54 years old.

In November after five long months of privation at sea he reached the barren coast of New Zealand, and the penal settlement of New Plymouth. Although he was pleased to be reunited with his son, he was shocked by the living conditions he found. The settlers had been promised a port and buildings against the money that they had invested, but no such work had been undertaken. Brown and Carlino lived in a primitive camp near the beach.

Within a few weeks he thought of returning home, to throw himself on the mercy of his friends. By December his health was deteriorating further. He sent letters of complaint to the New Plymouth Company. However his protests were ignored, and he was condemned for supposed ungentlemanly conduct. All fight evaporated, he was a broken man. He recalled Joseph Severn's invitation to come and live with him, and reminisced to whoever would listen about the halcyon days in Italy, and the time with literary friends at Hampstead – those men of letters, the actors, artists and singers, whose company and friendship he had enjoyed.

By February he felt he must sell his remaining investments to raise enough for the journey home. He wrote home telling of his plight. With a shaking hand he set down his feeling that he might not survive the journey. His agent in England failed to send any money. If he returned to England he would have to put his trust in the parish. Or finish his life here in the settlement. But then fate took over. On the 5th of June 1842 he suffered a fatal stroke. As he lay dying, a Baptist emigrant attempted to comfort him, asking that he turn to the Saviour for his salvation. "For the love of God, sir," retorted Brown, "Speak to me no more about that man!" To the very end, like his greatest friend the poet Keats, he died without religion.

As a deist, they refused to inter him within the consecrated churchyard. Carlino and Cooke, a friend of Edward Trelawny, followed the cortege up Marsland Hill. And there in the shadow of mount Taraniki lie the lonely remains of Charles Armitage-Brown, his memory ensured forever by his friendship with the poet John Keats.

A hundred years after he died, his grave had been forgotten, disappearing from sight during the Maori wars.

His relations searched for the grave, and men hacking away at the thick scrub on Marsland Hill struck a heavy stone. This stone carried a simple inscription:

"CHARLES BROWN" FRIEND OF KEATS

APPENDIX 1
(To Brown's letter dated the 21st of December 1820 to John Keats in Rome.)

Brown wrote about John Scott (1783–1821), editor of *The Morning Chronicle* and *London Magazine*. The letter went:

> "I know you don't like John Scott, but he is doing a thing that
> tickles me to the heart's core, and you will like to hear of it, if you
> have any revenge in your composition – By some means, 'crooked
> enough I dare say'. He has got possession of one of Blackwood's
> gang, who has turned King's evidence.

[Blackwood's *Edinburgh Magazine* The publication that had attacked Keats and his poems and his supposed membership of Leigh Hunt's 'Cockney School' of writers.]

> – Month after month he belabours them with the most damning facts that can be conceived; if they are indeed facts. I
> know not how the rogues can stand against them. This virulent
> attack has made me like the London magazine."

The person used by Scott for his supposed information against Blackwood's was J.H. Christie, Christie was a friend of John Lockhart assistant editor at Blackwood's who signed himself 'Z'. The quarrel between Scott and Christie grew out of all proportion, leading to one challenging the other to a duel. Which one made the challenge is not known, but the challenge was accepted and a duel took place at the end of February 1821 (a few days after the poet's own death in Rome). Neither of the men wanted death to be the outcome. However Christie's shot brought Scott to the ground where he died on the spot. Those at the time who knew Christie described him as a mild-mannered man who was devastated at the outcome.

APPENDIX 2

In the 1950s a Mrs Osborne the granddaughter of Brown wrote:

"My grandfather did not bring a big selection of his books to N.Z. The best I suppose, were his copies of Italian classics, which were leather bound. When we came to Auckland and were intending to go to South Africa a friend of my father's advised my mother to send the bulk of these books home to Christie's. He undertook the sending. Well the books were sent. We retained only those written by or connected with Keats, Shelley, Lamb, Hunt and so on.

All the Italian classics went. In the course of time, after expenses had been paid and the books sold, my mother received the sum of 7s.6d. That was, I suppose in the year 1902. I don't know if the books were sent to Christie's or to some other dealer. I don't suppose they could be traced now. Brown frequently pasted inside his books a visiting card with 'Mr Charles Brown' on it in copperplate. The friend who sent the books home was Dr John Logan Campbell. He may have sent them in the name of the Campbell Ehrenfried Company."

In another letter dated June 25th 1952, Mrs Osborne wrote:

"When my father died, we had a very thorough clearing up, heaps of things were burned, I mean papers, memos and so on. How much, we may ask was destroyed over those years, scraps and papers that would be valued today?"

John Keats
From a miniature by Joseph Severn, 1819
© *National Portrait Gallery, London*

Charles Cowden Clark
By an unknown artist.
© *National Portrait Gallery, London*

Charles Armitage-Brown
From a Bust by Andrew Wilson, 1828, Florence.
(Keats House, Hampstead)

Joseph Severn – aged 29
Self portrait
(Keats House, Hampstead)

The Clarke's School, Enfield, London.
Keats and his brothers, George and Tom,
educated here, 1803–1811
(From a watercolour by Mari Davey, 2012

Dr Hammond's House, Edmonton, London.
Keats served an apprenticeship here, 1811–1815
(From a watercolour by Mari Davey, 2010)

Wentworth Place (Keats House)
Hampstead, London.
(From a watercolour by Mari Davey, 1998)

The Mill House, Bedhampton, Sussex.
(From a watercolour by Mari Davey, 2007)

The Keats-Shelley Memorial House & Museum, Rome.
(From a watercolour by Mari Davey, 2008)

Keats on his deathbed.
A pen and ink drawing by Joseph Severn, 1821.
(Keats House, Hampstead)

IL CIMITERO ACATTOLICO DI ROMA
Keats' and Severn's graves.
(The Protestant Cemetery, Rome)

99

PART III

Joseph Severn
1793–1879

Landscape, Historical, and Portrait Painter,
celebrated for his miniatures of John Keats.

Joseph Severn was born on the 7th of December 1793 at
Hoxton, London, the eldest son of James Severn a musician.
At school Joseph had a recognised talent for sketching, and
was in demand by his fellows for his pencil portraits. On
leaving his education aged 14 he was apprenticed to William
Bond an engraver. Joseph did not take to the engraving, or
metal stabbing as he termed it. And having saved enough to
purchase an easel, brushes and paints left Bond early, then
with the support of his family set out on his own account. His
water colour miniature portraits were excellent and he was
soon earning a steady living from commissions. The Royal
Academy, recognising his undoubted talent, gave him a place
in their art school where he began using the more expensive
oil paint on classical canvases. In 1813 aged 20, he met
Keats and they became firm friends, a friendship that spurred
him with fresh ambition.

The Royal Academy ran a competition for its students; the
prize, a Gold Medal for the best historical painting. The
subject to be taken from Spenser. It was to be a large
painting and to purchase the required materials he sold his
watch and some books to raise enough to fund the work. The
picture he entered was entitled 'Una and the Red Cross
Knight in the Cave' (from Spenser's 'Cave of Despair'); the
picture won for him the Gold Medal. Another work of his at
about the same time 'Hermia and Helena' was accepted and
hung in an exhibition that year.

By now Severn had valuable friends about him, Leigh Hunt, John Reynolds, William Haslam, and Keats. This circle of writers, poets and business men served to improve his standing education and character. When in 1820 William Haslam suggested that he should go to Italy with Keats, a request to which he readily agreed he was maybe wiser than his family realised. For his father went to some lengths to dissuade his favourite son, believing that the venture would damage his future prospects. As it came about he was proved wrong.

At the time of his leaving England, Severn had begun work on a new picture 'The Death Of Alcibiades'. When Keats was ill and dying in Rome, he left off painting for his suffering friend's sake. It would be a while after the poet's death before he set to work to finish the picture.

The trial he experienced during the nursing of Keats became embedded in his mind, and this began to show in his later art. The picture 'The Death of Alcibiades' won him an award of £130 and The Royal Academy covered the expense of his visit to Rome.

Severn was an accomplished but not a great painter. He did not progress far with his art after his early success. However his portraits and miniatures of Keats are treasured, especially the earlier ones. Severn's work prospered for the sake of the poet whom he had supported with such devotion. It's possible that without this friendship with Keats he may have passed into obscurity.

Severn lived part of his life in Italy. In 1828 he married Elizabeth Montgomerie, the daughter of Lord Archibald Montgomerie. The couple had several children, three of whom themselves became artists of merit, one, Arthur Severn receiving a commission from Sir Percy Florence Shelley for a picture of the Coliseum at Rome, with his relation the poet Shelley in the foreground. Arthur was also involved with a planned illustrated edition of Shelley's

'Adonais' and a proposed portrait of Leigh Hunt, but neither of these commissions materialised.

In 1841 Severn returned to England and remained for a period of 19 years. In 1860 he became the British Consul at Rome. A position he held until 1872 when he retired with a pension from the British Government. He lived in Italy during his old age and died in Rome on the 3rd of August 1879 aged 85. Joseph Severn's last resting place is a grave next to that of his dearest friend John Keats, in the Old Protestant Cemetery Rome.

Joseph Severn, taller than Keats at five feet seven inches, was two years older than the poet. He was thin and a little effeminate in appearance, with dark almost Jewish features. His eyebrows, above wide-set brown eyes were heavy, with hair darker than that of his head. The hair of his head which he wore long, was a rich brown and naturally curly. His mouth with its ready smile, wide and full, set in a long thin face.

Although he seemed to lack confidence when meeting those he thought his superiors, he had a way of making people feel comfortable in his presence. He had a gift 'that Keats remarked on' of giving happiness to others.

Joseph Severn –Artist and friend of John Keats

Severn, with what seems to have been a well-known vagueness, dated his first meeting with Keats varying from 1813 to 1817. Severn became acquainted with John through his friendship with George Keats, who was employed as a clerk in the office of the Keats' guardian Richard Abbey, a tea importer. George had time to socialise and was well-known as a man about town, he was well liked, gregarious and generous and had a wide circle of friends.

Keats serving his apprenticeship at Guy's Hospital had little time free from his work and studies. He lived in shared lodgings with other students, and it wasn't until 1817 when he abandoned medicine and blossomed onto the literary world, that he began to make new friends beyond those of his hospital environment. Severn was one of Keats' earliest artistic friends, coming into the poet's life before Leigh Hunt. And it was Severn who brought to the circle another young man, the lawyer William Haslam, whom the Keats' brothers later described as "our oak friend".

Severn's friendship with Keats opened up a whole new world for the young artist. And now free from the drudgery of a seven-year apprenticeship to what he termed 'metal stabbing' (engraving), he turned with renewed vigour to painting. The friendship with Keats lifted him, and he prepared to make a fresh beginning. Whilst apprenticed he had attended art classes at night, but for the most part was self-taught. In his spare time he painted miniatures, portraits, which he sold for ten shillings and six pence and used the money to buy more art materials. By the time of his early acquaintance with Keats he had developed quite a prosperous small business with his miniature painting.

In the summer of 1817 the two friends were close, spending many hours walking on Hampstead Heath. Keats, a keen observer in his own right, drew on the painter's insight, and Severn listened intently as Keats spoke on literature, history and Greek mythology. We are indebted to Severn for his description of the poet as he approached his twenty-first birthday. Severn noted that although Keats was small, little more than three quarters of an inch over five feet, he seemed taller, partly because of the erect carriage of his limbs and head, and the almost perfect proportions of his body. But mostly because of his facial expression which Severn described as dauntless; "Such as may be seen on the face of some seamen. Only when deep in thought or reading was his stature noticeable. His eyes, hazel and gypsy-coloured, impressed everyone. They seemed to glow and almost throw out a light of their own in front of him. Just like those of certain birds that habitually front the sun." (Keats' hawk-like appearance was softened and not noticeable in the Severn portraits.) "His complexion was bright and glowing, his features quivering and mobile. He had a large mouth with a jutting upper lip and this gave him a slightly pugnacious appearance, but this was not enough to spoil the overall impression of a head described as that of a Greek god. His hair was reddish gold, naturally wavy and alive; the long silken curls hung like the rich plumage of a bird."

However there was another side to the poet; although Severn proved unreliable on facts and dates, his observations were accurate. He was one of the few people outside Keats' own family to record the other side to Keats' character.

Keats suffered moods when all life drained from him. He would become nervous and depressed, and seemed to his friends to be the complete opposite of his usual attractive self. This change could come about suddenly and marked the onset of what he recognised as his own black moods. He became suspicious, irrational, brooding over small faults and problems. In his own words they became "a theme for

Sophocles". At these times, Severn noted, "He would answer harshly and coldly or not speak at all, and his eyes, the only part of his face to seem alive, would darken and veil themselves in shadows as if consumed by some secret and fatal anguish. These depressive mood swings were sometimes damaging to his friendships."

Although Keats was for the most part tolerant of his friend's faults, by the end of his life there was not one of them that had not disillusioned him at one time or another. In his letters he would recriminate, and then retract with an apology for what he termed his "lunes". His friends and close family forgave this as being part of his natural behaviour which did not detract from, and may have even enhanced, his nature.

Whilst Keats had been away from London in 1817 at the Isle of Wight, searching for inspiration and beginning his epic poem 'Endymion', Severn pestered his brother George as to when John would be returning.

In the latter part of that summer Severn attached himself to Keats, accompanying him on his long walks. Taking advantage of the good weather that year, the two friends set out across Hampstead Heath to Caen Wood and still further, far into the Middlesex Forest. Severn found Keats' taste in the arts, his knowledge of history and mythology fascinating, and as Severn was not well-read the knowledge that he obtained from Keats was a valuable addition to his education. Keats suggested subjects from historical literature for Severn to use in his paintings, the type of pictures that were in vogue at the time. Severn had already exhibited one, 'Una and the Red Cross Knight in the Cave'.

Joseph Severn recorded the power that Keats seemed to have to enter into the identity of everything around him. "Nothing seemed to escape him, the song of a bird, the rustle of some animal in the hedgerow, the changing colours, light and shadow, the motion of grasses to the wind, how it moved tall plants and flowers, and the movement of cloud across the sky. The gestures and features of passing humanity, the colour of a woman's hair, a child's smile, the hidden mystery of the tramps and vagrants, even hats, shoes, clothes, whatever might reveal something of the wearer." Severn in turn helped to shape Keats' knowledge of the arts, with visits to art galleries, and exhibitions. Their talks on ancient Greece, the enjoyment of Greek mythology, all found their way into his epic poem, 'Endymion'.

Little correspondence between Severn and Keats survives, some is likely to have been lost. But on the other hand Keats did not write long letters to Severn, and that which is lost may be of little importance, being in the form of short notes. On the weekend of June the 6th 1818 the two had arranged a meeting; Keats was unwell, with a recurrence of his sore throat, and sent a note to Severn to put him off:

Address: Mr Joseph Severn. Islington Road, Near the Angel Inn.

Postmark: 6 Ju 1818.

My dear Severn,
   The Doctor says I mustn't go out. I wish such a delicious fate would put me in cue to entertain you with a Sonnet or a Pun.

I am, yours ever
John Keats

The address could have been that of William Bond the engraver, who had his business in Islington Road, however it's believed that Severn's apprenticeship had by this time been terminated.

The content of the next letter places it before the Royal Academy exhibition of 1819, in which the miniature portrait of Keats and the picture 'Hermia and Helena' were on public display. In the catalogue the portrait was number 940 and the picture 267.

Wentworth Place
Monday-aft-

My dear Severn,

Your note gave me some pain, not on my own
account, but on yours – Of course I should never suffer
any petty vanity of mine to hinder you in any wise; and
therefore I should say put the miniature in the
exhibition if only myself was to be hurt. But, will it not
hurt you? What good can it do to any future picture.
Even a large picture is lost in that canting place – what
a drop of water in the ocean is a Miniature.

Those who might chance to see it for the most part
if they had ever heard of either of us – and know what
we were and of what years would laugh at the puff of
the one and the vanity of the other. I am however in
these matters a very bad judge – and would advise you
to act in a way that appears to yourself the best for
your interest. As your Hermia and Helena is finished
send that without the prologue of a Miniature. I shall
see you soon, if you do not pay me a visit sooner –
there's a Bull for you.

Yours ever sincerely
John Keats

The next letter was, it seems, written more than seven
months on from the March one. It has been assumed that it
belongs to October 1819; Keats wrote Wednesday, but the
date is missing. He is still referring to one of Severn's
pictures, although he does not title it, but we know that it was
of 'The Cave of Despair'. The Severn family must have
moved again. The number is 6 not 19 Frederick Place,
Goswell Street.

Address: Joseph Severn Esq. 6 Goswell Street Road, Opposite Spencer Street. Postmark. Hampstead. [no date]

Wentworth Place. Wednesday.

Dear Severn,

Either your Joke about staying at home is a very old one or I really call'd. I don't remember doing so. I am glad to hear you have finish'd the Picture and am more anxious to see it than I have time to spare: for I have been so very lax, unemployed, unmeridian'd, and objectless these two months that I even grudge indulging (and that is no great indulgence considering the Lecture is not over till 9 and the lecture room seven miles from Wentworth Place) myself by going to Hazlitt's Lecture. [Hazlitt's lectures on the Dramatic Literature of the Elizabethan Age, at the Surrey Institution, Blackfriars Road] If you have hours to the amount of a brace of dozens to throw away you may sleep nine of them here in your little Crib and chat the rest – When your Picture is up and in a good light I shall make a point of meeting you at the Academy if you will let me know when.

If you should be at the Lecture tomorrow evening I shall see you – and congratulate you heartily – Haslam I know "is very Beadle to an amorous sigh" [quote from *Love's Labour's Lost*].

Your sincere friend
John Keats.

In November 1818, Keats was out of circulation. The reason for this was his constant nursing of Tom, the younger brother who now approached the final stage of tuberculosis, and had one month left to live.

The Academy Exhibition of that year must have been postponed, for on the 17th of November Queen Charlotte died. Regency London was plunged into mourning; theatres and places of public entertainment were closed. (Charlotte, Queen to King George the 3rd from 1761. Charlotte – 1744–1818, mother of fifteen children.)

Severn himself had been unwell, but had recovered enough by the middle of November to visit Keats at Well Walk, Hampstead, where the brothers lodged with Bentley the postman. He found Tom dying, and was shocked to see how much Keats had suffered by the constant care of his sick brother. Theatres and the galleries reopened on the 3rd of December, Keats himself now mourning his brother who had died on the 1st. The burial of Thomas Keats took place at St Stephen's, Coleman Street on the 7th of December 1818.

The last letter that we have from Keats to Severn was dated December 1819, the date unclear, but said to be the 6th. It is sent from Wentworth Place, Hampstead. (Keats by now was lodging with Charles Brown.)

My dear Severn,
I am very sorry that on Tuesday I have an appointment in the City of an undeferable nature; and Brown on the same day has some business at Guildhall. I have not been able to figure your manner of executing the Cave of despair, therefore it will be at any rate a novelty and surprise to me, I trust on the right side. I shall call upon you some morning shortly early enough to catch you before you can get out – when we will proceed to the Academy. I think you must be suited with a good painting light in your Bay window. I wish you to return the Compliment by going with me to see a Poem I have hung up for the Prize in the Lecture Room of the Surrey Institution. I have many Rivals the most threatening are – An Ode to Lord Castereagh, and a new series of Hymns for the new, New Jerusalem Chapel – you had best put me into your Cave of despair –

Ever yours sincerely
John Keats

In Severn's relics there was an outside page of a letter bearing a Hampstead postmark, addressed to Joseph Severn Esq., 6 Goswell Street Road, Near Northampton Square. This frontispiece is likely to belong to this letter written by Keats on Monday the 6th of December 1819.

The pictures for the 'Cave of Despair' competition were to be in the Academy by the 1st of November 1819. A journalist from the *Literary Gazette* had seen them by the 10th of December, the day on which the prizes were to be awarded. This critic at the time of his article did not know the names of the recipients, but praised the entry of a Mr Severn "Who has produced a very clever and unexaggerated picture." This painting appeared at the Academy exhibition for 1820. In the Annals of the Fine Arts appeared a note on it:

"This picture, it appears, obtained the medal last year; we are sorry that of all their students such as this should be the best. Their regulations drive the able from their schools, and humble mediocrity is all that is left them."

In the Academy catalogue for 1820 the title of the picture is 'Una and the Red Cross Knight in the Cave'. The number of the entry was 398.

The idea for the work came from Spenser's *The Faerie Queen*, where Una seizes a dagger from the Red Cross Knight to prevent his using it against himself. The reference to the painting in the 'Annals of the Fine Arts' was meant as a joke.

When Fanny Brawne came into Keats' life in 1819, she, like girls are apt to do, threw all his plans into disarray, if in fact he had any firm plans. In a letter to Haydon in December he spoke of a wish to travel for the purpose of his studies, subject to having enough money. All of Keats' friends seem to have taken a dislike to Fanny. It is probable that in this dislike there was an element of jealousy. A man is seldom satisfied with his friend's choice of a lover, and Keats' friends had a very strong attraction to him. Severn thought her a "cold and calculating mistress" but this did not stop him flirting with her, or her with him, much to the annoyance of Keats.

From June 1819 to the October, Keats cut himself off from Fanny Brawne and his London friends and went off to work at his poetry in the Isle of Wight and Winchester with Charles Brown. Short of money he returned to London, planning to write for his living. He didn't want to return to Brown and the protective closeness of Wentworth Place. Dilke found him lodgings in a quiet house near to his own at College Street, Westminster. His mind was unsettled, full of Fanny Brawne and Wentworth Place, and he found it impossible to work.

Severn visited him soon after his arrival in town. He had expected to find his friend in better health after his long break in the country, however he was to be disappointed; Keats looked ill. However he was in good spirits and full of his poetry. The evening spent with Keats was delightful. The poet went on and on, showing one new poem after another.

'Hyperion' affected him so much that he remembered the work for the rest of his life. He urged Keats to finish the poem, and then made the mistake of comparing its style to that of Milton.

An angry Keats retorted, "That is just the point; I do not wish to put my name to a poem that might have been written by John Milton, but one that is unquestionably the work of John Keats." Severn didn't like 'Lamia', he thought it strange that Keats' genius should be taken up by a rhyming story about a serpent changing its form into that of a girl. He said that he would return another night if Keats would read the poem aloud. He would reserve final judgement until then. During the next two weeks Severn was busy painting, and when he finally found time to return to College Street, Keats had gone back to Hampstead, taking up his old lodgings with Charles

Brown at Wentworth Place. Now just a wall separated him from the distraction of Miss Fanny Brawne.

In May 1819, Keats found time for another visit to view Severn's paintings, now hanging at Somerset House. Near to his own miniature portrait there hung Isabella Jones's new head and shoulders miniature by A.E. Chalon, a reminder of her beauty, and his strong attraction for her, now dead and in the past. John Taylor his publisher had told him that Isabella was unwell and gone to Tunbridge Wells looking for an improvement in her health. The same month a letter from George in America arrived. It contained disquieting news of business failure and financial problems. And now Keats himself felt unwell. Whilst at Winchester he had thrown himself into work, but his brief spell of mental brilliance had faded.

In January 1820 King George the 3rd died. The spirit in Keats was also dying. Brown was worried about his friend – the play that they had written together, which was to have made their fortune, (*Otho the Great*) had been accepted at Drury Lane Theatre, but mainly due to Brown's impatience it was never put on. Severn was however riding high, he had won the coveted Academy Gold Medal, and Keats rejoiced at his friend's success.

On February the 3rd the beast of consumption reared – Keats had his first lung haemorrhage. Taylor and Hessey his publishers urged him to prepare his poems for a new book. John struggled to find an interest in anything. During his return to England on the money raising quest, George took the opportunity to copy out all of the poems that he had not seen. Among those he copied were the four great odes which, strangely, Keats had failed to mention in his letters to America. On a cold snowy morning, George copied out one which he later described as particularly moving – 'Ode to a Nightingale'. Keats read it over to him in his usual monotone, with little inflection in his voice. The room was extremely cold; Keats jokingly said, "This is like reading an account of the black hole at Calcutta on an iceberg!"

Many years on, Severn told a moving story on how the nightingale ode came into being. One spring evening in 1919, Keats, and a group of his friends, including Severn, were at 'The Spaniard's Inn' on Hampstead Heath. As dusk fell Severn realised that Keats was no longer with them, on going out to look for him, he found Keats lying up on a little hill under a group of pines known as Constable's Firs, listening to a nightingale. John was moved and delighted by the song of the bird, whose mate had a nest in the garden of Wentworth Place. The next morning he sat for three hours under the plum tree in the garden, returning to the house with two sheets of paper in his hand. Brown, coming in at the same time, watched as Keats put them behind some books, not wanting his friend to see the rough draft of what was in fact the 'Ode to a Nightingale'. Brown's close attention to Keats' work must at time have annoyed him. But without Brown's dedication much of the poet's work could well have been lost, for as he said, "Keats wrote on any scrap of paper that came to hand, putting it aside, not troubling much more about it."

In the summer of 1920 Severn saw very little of Keats. He knew that he was ill, but had no knowledge of just how invasive the sickness in fact was. Keats was being nursed by Mrs Brawne and Fanny. Severn thought that this situation could only improve his health. The artist had little free time from his painting and the light of the summer hours had to be used to the full. When he did go to see Keats at Wentworth Place, he was shocked to find that John had declined since their last meeting.

In the July when Keats was lodging with Leigh Hunt, his health had deteriorated to a dangerous level. Hunt called in Doctor William Lamb, a man of somewhat unusual appearance, an eccentric vegetarian and albino, whose pale appearance must have startled Keats. For a second opinion

Lamb called in his friend and consultant Doctor George Darling. Both men agreed that if Keats was to have any chance of recovery he must leave the country. Another English winter would surely kill him. Hunt got his friends together and it was decided that John should go to Italy. It took some time to arrange, the biggest problem being finance. Charles Brown was away walking in the north, and Haslam had just married.

Finally it fell to Taylor and Hessey the publishers to make the arrangements. An agreement was drawn up between Keats and his publishers for the rights to all his poems, and they advanced the necessary funds. A sum of £150 guaranteed to a bank in Rome was for the expenses of Keats and whoever would go with him, and would last just over two months if they were frugal. Most of his friends made contributions to the cost of the passage and immediate needs. George in America promised reimbursement at a later date.

Who was to accompany Keats? Brown, the first choice, would maybe have gone. But it would certainly have been an embarrassment to him in his financial state at the time. However Brown had vanished into the north and letters sent received no reply.

Joseph Severn was suggested, and as time was indeed short it was agreed that Haslam would approach him on the subject. On the thirteenth of September Haslam called on Severn. He found the painter at work in his lodgings. After telling him the situation with regard to Keats he asked, "Will you go?" Severn had not travelled far from London's streets, and the prospect of going to Italy must have seemed to him alarming. However, assured on a few important points, one being finance, he answered there and then, "Yes, I'll go." Discussions soon led him to think that a winter in Rome might be of benefit to his painting; and as the holder of an Academy Gold Medal he was entitled to apply for a travelling scholarship. It was every artist's dream to go to Italy. A picture from there, if accepted by the Academy, would possibly win him the award of a hundred and thirty pounds, and with it the leisure of three years to paint what he liked.

But, if on the other hand there had been the prospect of little or no benefit for himself, he would still have been willing to go. His dearest friend was in need, and that was in itself enough. But as it was, he was about give up his livelihood after a three-year struggle building a reputation. He had very little savings, but had just received a payment of twenty-five pounds for a miniature, or else he must have gone on borrowed money. A few personal items and his painting equipment were soon packed, and the next morning he returned his keys to the landlord, then went home to break the news to his family.

A passport had to be applied for, after which he visited Sir Thomas Lawrence, requesting introductions in Rome. Sir Thomas readily obliged and wished him well. His spirits rose.

But at home there was trouble. His mother, who he called an 'Angel', fully understood, and together with his sisters she undertook to prepare his travelling trunk. His father however reproached him. He was a man of quick temper, but Severn loved him, as he loved all his family. Parting from them was to be hard enough without the disapproval of his father. Mr Severn could not understand that his eldest son would see a friend's claim on him greater that that of his own family. Keats was even then with Taylor in Fleet Street, tying loose ends, awaiting the call to board the *Maria Crowther* as soon as the brig would be ready to sail.

It was late into the night of the 16th when Severn went home to collect his trunk and say his final goodbyes. The coach waited at the door. As he entered he found his mother in tears and his father slumped down in his armchair, a picture of grief and misery. The heavy trunk stood in the middle of the room. His sisters watched, fighting their own emotions.

Severn's heart sank, the parting was to be more difficult than he had imagined. Severn and his brother Tom had difficulty getting the heavy trunk though the door to the waiting carriage; he was forced to ask his father for help who rose from his chair in a temper, swearing that if without his help the trunk could not be lifted, it would never be lifted at all, and would never be touched by him. Severn was forced to request help from the coachman. When the trunk was stowed, and with his father still raving, Severn kept his peace, and went up the stairs to say goodbye to his youngest brother. As he came down his father barred the door, and when his son attempted to pass, knocked him to the floor. Tom Severn, a powerful young man of nineteen, had to use all his strength to restrain the angry father while his brother passed through. There was no time for a reconciliation, Severn went, leaving sorrow and upset behind him.

Tom was to accompany his brother to the dock, and then as far as Gravesend. The brothers sat together in gloomy silence as the coach made its way slowly through the darkness. Severn was, in addition to the pain of the distressful parting, unwell with a liver complaint. But as they neared the south bank of the Thames with the ships' masts, dark lines etched in the sky of a pale dawn, his spirits rose. He was at the beginning of a new life. And the friend he loved the most waited at the wharf with Taylor, Haslam, Woodhouse and other friends. By Taylor's side was William Smith, his apprentice who would act as runner should any last minute emergencies arise. Maybe it was this young man who in 1827, using the pen-name of 'Gaston', had some verses published in *Hone's Table Book* describing Keats at the dockside that morning.

> Still do I see thee on the river's strand
> Take thy last step upon thy native land –
> Still I feel the last kind pressure of thy hand.
> A calm dejection in thy youthful face,
> To which e'en sickness lent a tender grace –

A hectic bloom – the sacrificial flower
Which marks the approach of Death's
all-withering power.

The *Maria Crowther*, a small brigantine of 127 tons, cast off from London Docks at seven o'clock a.m., on Sunday the 17th of September. Taylor, Woodhouse, Haslam and Tom Severn went on board with Keats. On the way down the river, Severn remembered his passport which had not arrived before he left. Haslam promised to get it, and that he would bring it to the ship before it sailed. Keats' friends must have had misgivings when they saw the quarters that were to be home for Keats and Severn during what was likely to be a long voyage.

The *Maria Crowther* had but one cabin for passengers, the ship's captain also used part of the space as his night cabin. The only privacy provided was by curtains along the bunks. Whilst the ship was still in the London docks a middle-aged woman came aboard. Mrs Pigeon seemed at first to be a cheerful enough little person, but was not overly pleased when she realised that she must share the cramped cabin with two young men with just a curtain screen to preserve her dignity.

The ship had left the London Dock early that morning to make its way to a new anchorage at Gravesend, arriving at about midday. Excepting for Haslam, who left the ship to get Severn's passport, the other friends remained aboard until the evening. At six o'clock Haslam returned with the passport. Before the friends parted, Keats wrote a short note which he handed to Taylor. It was maybe intended for Fanny Brawne. Some of the note is surely missing, for its brevity makes little sense – "The passport arrived before we started. I don't think I shall be long ill. God bless you – farewell. John Keats." Taylor wrote a letter for Fanny Keats, which Haslam promised to deliver by hand. Taylor wrote:

"He did not go ashore but entered at once on the kind of life which he will have to lead for about a Month to come. Dining in the Cabin with the Captain, and another passenger a lady' besides Severn, the Friend who is gone with him – The Vessel waited at Gravesend for another Lady who was coming on board there. Mr Taylor, Mr Haslam and Mr Woodhouse accompanied Mr Keats to Gravesend, and left him at four o'clock on Sunday afternoon. – He was then comfortably settled in his new Habitation with every prospect of having a pleasant Voyage. – His Health was already much improved by the air of the River, by the Exercise and the amusement which the sailing afforded. He was provided with everything that would contribute to make the Time pass agreeably, and with all that his Health required."

Taylor composed the letter, but it was written by another hand, whose we don't know. The letter painted a rosy picture for the benefit of Keats' worried young sister. Fanny Keats had been forbidden a farewell visit to her brother by the restrictive Abbey family and in her heart she felt that she would never see him again.

The letter painted a false picture indeed, for the brig was poorly equipped, its sails and running gear well worn. The provisions although adequate made no pretence on the side of luxury. As Haslam prepared to leave the ship he took Severn aside, requesting him to keep a journal and write letters describing the voyage and their life abroad for the benefit of Keats' friends. Severn agreed, and it is from his records and letters written at the time that we obtain the details of Severn's life with Keats over the last months of the poet's life.

As he was about to make his goodbyes, Richard Woodhouse slipped a letter into Keats' hand, a letter making a generous promise. Woodhouse wrote; though at present he was short of money, it would give him great satisfaction later to answer a draft of his for "there is no one who would be more welcome than yourself to share my little Superfluities."

He asked for a lock of his friend's hair. William Haslam promised to call on Fanny Keats and to give her a personal account of her brother's departure; he would report to both Fanny Keats and Brawne that Keats' health and spirits were better at the beginning of the momentous voyage than anyone could have expected.

The letter that Taylor wrote, which Haslam took to Fanny Keats, says that Taylor, Haslam and Woodhouse left the *Maria Crowther* at four o'clock on the Sunday afternoon. This is in doubt, for other letters of the time record; 'Excepting Haslam, who left the ship to get Severn's passport, the other friends remained aboard until the evening. At six o'clock p.m., Haslam returned with Severn's passport, and before the friends parted Keats wrote a short note.'

That evening during tea in the cabin, Keats cracked a few jokes and seemed quite his old self. But very soon became overcome with tiredness and the effects of the wine drunk during the farewells. He and Severn were soon fast asleep, and when morning came Mrs Pidgeon complained about their snoring. Severn was shocked awake several times by bad dreams – the first, in a shoemaker's shop hearing the sound of hammers against leather, in the next, he found himself in a wine cellar that was half filled with water.

During the night a Scottish coastal smack made its way into the anchorage and dropped its own anchor almost alongside the gently rocking *Maria Crowther*. On board Charles Armitage Brown, Keats' best friend and landlord of Wentworth Place! On receipt of the letter containing the news of Keats' departure for Italy Brown had boarded the first available vessel from Dundee. As a new day dawned, he urged the smack's skipper to weigh anchor, he was eager to get to Hampstead to see Keats and find out what his plans were. As the little vessel moved swiftly upriver on an incoming tide, Brown fretted impatiently for arrival at the London wharf. Then he hurried to Hampstead, only to be informed by Fanny Brawne that he had missed Keats by just a day. Both Keats and Brown were to realise later what a cruel trick fate had played on them; for during the night the anchored smack had been just a few yards from a sleeping Keats aboard the *Maria Crowther*.

Thomas Walsh the captain of the brig was a caring man, anxious to make his passengers as comfortable as possible. After breakfast on the 18th, he and Severn went ashore to do last minute shopping. They purchased, among other provisions, fresh fruit, bread and biscuits. Captain Walsh tried to buy a goat, thinking to provide fresh milk for the invalids – goat's milk being especially good for the well being of those with problems of the chest. Keats gave Severn a list of items to buy from the chemists, and on this list was one item in particular – a bottle of laudanum, the heroin-based liquid used for pain relief.

In the late afternoon the ship's little group of passengers sat down to a meal with the captain. Keats had found an appetite and ate well. He was in high spirits and looked better. Miss Cotterell, the last passenger came on board. She was a ladylike, slim pretty girl. But John was shocked to find that she was a consumptive and like himself going to Italy to escape the winter, also looking to improve her health. She was naturally apprehensive by the prospect of a difficult and lonely voyage. The two young men did their best to cheer her up. Severn tried to keep up with Keats, but said; "My wit would have dropped in a minute but for Keats plying me, but I was done up for all that, leaving him soul master. I struck up again in my own language or Keats would have borne the lady off in triumph." Severn was worn out, his face pallid, the skin yellow from his liver complaint. And he was still troubled by the trauma of parting from his family. A friend of Miss Cotterell came to see her off and asked which of the two was the dying man? Severn was also beginning to feel seasick, and this before the voyage had really begun. He said "that as a matter of course his dinner would always come again to light!"

That evening the little ship lifted its anchor and made its way seaward on the last of the ebb tide. Keats took to his bunk exhausted, while Severn sat up on deck till midnight, sketching the moonlight on the water. Now as they proceeded along the Kentish coast the wind began to freshen. Next day the storm had come on in earnest although the wind came from a favourable quarter driving them on past Margate. All of the passengers were seasick and could take nothing more than weak tea all day. Miss Cotterell fainted away. All took to their bunks too weak to remove their clothing. Sleep was impossible, but Keats spurred by necessity and to relieve his own feelings made himself doctor and prescribed for the others from his bunk.

On Wednesday the 20th of September, and off Brighton, the weather was bright and calm. Keats however told Severn that he felt uneasy, as he had experienced similar weather conditions on his last visit to this coastline. "I believe that more bad weather will very soon arrive; this is a calm before the storm." The wind began to freshen and veered round, building to a force six south-westerly, blowing into the teeth of the *Maria Crowther*'s course. During the afternoon the ship was pounded by heavy seas. As daylight faded a plank sprang in the side, and the cabin soon flooded. The passengers' belongings washed from side to side with the violent movement. The women in their bunks were terrified. Severn got down from his bunk to find water half way up his calves. "Here's pretty music for you," Severn's voice faltered! "Yes," was Keats' calm reply, "water parted from the sea," quoting from a popular song of the day by 'Arne'. Captain Walsh, seeing the extent of the damage, decided to stop trying to make way against the wind and the tide that had also turned against them, and put the ship about. A manoeuvre accomplished with some difficulty, to run before the storm.

After a worrying night, the dawn found passengers and crew exhausted. And the ship twenty miles back off Dungeness and New Romney. The weather abated, and by contrast for the next two days the *Maria Crowther* rocked gently from side to side, becalmed. Captain Walsh ordered the long boat lowered, allowing the passengers ashore for a while. Keats and Severn took advantage of the offer and tramped along the shingle of Dungeness, arousing the suspicion of an excise officer who questioned them as to their intentions. The two ladies kept to the ship; Mrs Pidgeon sat on deck, whilst the sickly Miss Cotterell lay exhausted in her bunk.

Keats had shown no sign of weakness of a spiritual nature, neither did he complain during this trying adventure. However, in spite of his previous forced cheerfulness, the days at sea had taken their toll on him. Severn noticed a change for the worse – John became irritable closed up in the tiny cabin, and rejected the dull food. He complained on the dampness of his bunk. He was feverish and distressed by the fact that in Miss Cotterell he saw mirrored his own complaint. Every symptom of her tuberculosis was a reminder of his own. After ten days in the English Channel, being battered by the elements this way and that, Captain Walsh knew that he must put his ship into port for repairs, and use the opportunity to take on board extra provisions. Putting into Portsmouth he informed his passengers that the ship would stay in harbour for at least two days.

Keats realised that the Snooks, the friendly miller and his wife, were just a few miles away at Bedhampton. Severn readily agreed that a break from the ship would do both of them some good, and that afternoon they took a coach the seven miles to the Mill House, where Keats had written his romantic poem 'The Eve of St Agnes'. John and Laetitia Snook were surprised to see Keats and his friend crunching across the gravel toward their front door. The Snooks knew nothing at the time of Keats' journey to Italy. They welcomed the travellers warmly, and as they all sat at the evening supper table, Keats gave them a lively account of their adventures so far.

The Snooks also had some surprising news of their own – Charles Brown had returned from Scotland, and was even now just ten miles away at Chichester, staying with the elderly Dilkes. John felt tempted to make the short journey to Chichester there and then. He would say his personal goodbye to the man he considered his best friend. Later he would find out how close they had been when the smack with Brown aboard had passed the *Maria Crowther* at Gravesend on its way up to London. John was now presented with a chance to end the voyage and return to Wentworth Place. Secretly, Severn hoped that he might do so. A visit to Brown might make up his mind one way or the other. That night in the bed where he had slept during his last visit to the Mill House, in the very room that the 'Eve of St Agnes' had been composed, he became convinced that the journey should be completed. Suppose he should return to London, what good would it do? He would take with him his tubercle lungs and worse! It came to him whatever he did the ending would be the same. To return now with Brown to Wentworth Place and Fanny would be certain death; however, the journey continued might just have a very slim chance of his survival at its end. Keats spent his last night in England twisting and turning, both body and mind in the back bedroom of the Mill House near Langstone Harbour Bedhampton. After breakfast with their genial hosts, Keats and Severn returned to the *Maria Crowther* which set sail once more on the afternoon of Friday the 29th of September.

Off Yarmouth, Isle of Wight, the ship was yet again becalmed, and Keats nerved himself to write a letter to Brown. A letter he felt he must write while the little strength he had remained.

To Charles Brown. Saturday Sept 30th 1820
Address: Mr Charles Brown, Wentworth Place,
Hampstead, Middx.

[Keats then must have mixed his dates for he begins
the letter:]

Saturday Sept 28th
Maria Crowther
off Yarmouth. Isle of Wight.

My Dear Brown,

The time has not yet come for a pleasant Letter from me. I have delayed writing to you from time to time because I felt how impossible it was to enliven you with one heartening hope of my recovery; this morning in bed the matter struck me in a different manner; I thought I would write 'While I was in some Liking' [Shakespeare's – *Henry IV*] or I might become too ill to write at all, and then if the desire to have written should become strong it would be a great affliction to me. I have many more letters to write and I bless my stars that I have begun, – this may be my best opportunity. We are in a calm and I am easy enough this morning. If my spirits seem too low you may in some degree impute it to our having been at sea a fortnight without making any way. I was very disappointed at not meeting you at Bedhampton, and am very provoked at the thought of you being at Chichester today. [Of course Brown was at Chichester on the 28th which was the Thursday] I should have delighted in setting off for London for the sensation merely – for what should I do there? I could not leave my lungs or stomach or other worse things behind me. I wish I could write on subjects that will not agitate me much – there is one I must mention and have done with it. Even if my body would recover of itself, this would prevent it. The very thing which I want to live most for will be a great occasion of my death. I cannot help it. Who can help it? Were I in health it would make me ill, and how can I bear it in my state? I dare say you will guess on what subject I am harping – you know what was my greatest pain during the first part of my illness at your house. I wish for death every day and night to deliver me from these pains, and then I wish death away, for death would destroy even those pains which are better than nothing. Land and sea, weakness and decline are great separators, but death is the great divorcer forever. When the pang of this thought has passed through my mind, I may say the bitterness of death is passed.

I often wish for you that you might flatter me with the best. I think without mentioning it for my sake you would be a friend to Miss Brawne when I am dead. You think she has many faults – but, for my sake, think she has not one – if there is any thing you can do for her by word or deed I know you will do it. I am in a state at present in which woman merely as woman can have no more power over me than stocks and stones, and yet the difference of my sensations with respect to Miss Brawne and my Sister is amazing. The one seems to absorb the other to a degree incredible. I seldom think of my Brother and Sister – in America. The thought of leaving Miss Brawne is beyond every thing horrible – the sense of darkness coming over me – I eternally see her figure eternally vanishing. Some of the phases she was in the habit of using during my last nursing at Wentworth Place ring in my ears. Is there another Life? Shall I awake and find this a dream? There must be we cannot be created for this sort of suffering. The receiving this letter is to be one of yours. I will say nothing about our friendship or rather yours to me more than that as you deserve to escape you will never be so unhappy as I am. I should think of – you in my last moments. I shall endeavour to write to Miss Brawne if possible to day. [He never did, or write to her ever again.] A sudden stop to my life in the

126

middle of one of these Letters would be no bad thing for it keeps one in a sort of fever awhile. Though fatigued with a Letter longer than any I have written for a long while it would be better to go on for ever than to wake to a sense of contrary winds. We expect to put into Portland roads to night. The Captain the Crew and the Passengers are all ill-tempered and weary. I shall write to Dilke. I feel as if I was closing my last letter to you. – My dear Brown

Your affectionate friend
John Keats

Their hopes of a good start to the voyage were soon dashed. Next day the ship was becalmed off the Dorset coast. The long boat swung out again, taking Keats and Severn ashore at Lulworth Cove. The excitement at the beginning of the journey had long since faded into abject misery brought about by the shear frustration of not being able to get away from the shoreline. But now with his feet on solid land Keats began to recover from his despair. Severn felt a senses of relief as they explored the caverns and grottoes; the fissures of Stair Hole and Durdle Door. That night, back on board, Severn saw Keats with a pen poring over the sonnet 'Bright Star'. He was delighted, believing that the poet had recovered enough to begin writing again. The first draft of this work had however been set down some two years earlier. John said nothing when Severn requested a copy, he just took up a pencil and wrote the sonnet on a blank page of the folio of Shakespeare's poems that he had been reading, and gave it to Severn. At length the *Maria Crowther* edged away from the shore and sailed out past Land's End into the Bay of Biscay.

They soon ran into heavy seas, and the portholes were closed for hour after hour. Miss Cotterell was becoming visibly weaker and many times fainted completely away. She and Keats reacted one to the other to the detriment of both. Severn, feeling a little better, escaped to the deck where his painter's eyes took in the magnificence of the skies and the long curling waves. He was amazed at the way the little ship rode the seas, shouldering up the steep waves to rush again down at the other side. Off Cape St Vincent the wind fell away and the ship was again becalmed. Sitting out on deck in warm sunshine, the two friends read to each other in turn. The book was Byron's *Don Juan*, and when Keats came to Byron's account of the shipwreck he threw the book aside in disgust, condemning what he called Byron's "Paltry originality, that of being new by making solemn things gay and gay things solemn." Byron had enjoyed more success than Keats. *Child Harold* had sold more than a thousand copies in less than a month. Whereas Keats' new book of poems was struggling to move from the shelves. "What it is to be five foot tall and not a lord," he had exclaimed. Byron had savagely criticised Keats' poems, and there was little love lost between the two.

Again John drifted into one of his black depressions, and to Severn's horror, now revealed his reason for asking him to purchase the laudanum. It was not to be used as a medicine, he wished to end the misery of his life by suicide. He knew all too well the effects of the disease and was by now without hope of recovery. He felt the growing weakness, the increasing dependence on others. Severn pleaded with him and managed to divert his purpose for the time being. As the breeze picked up, the ship slowly regained its course and a school of dolphins played at the bow. Severn called to Keats when he noticed a whale in the distance spouting from its blowhole. As the idyllic afternoon wore on, the serenity of the situation helped John to regain his composure.

This period of serenity was not to last, for the next day the little brig found itself approached by two large Portuguese men-of-war. At first the vessels were the subject of interest; the passengers and some of the crew went to the rail for a better view of the nearest ship, the *San Josef* a four-decker that dwarfed the 127 ton *Maria Crowther*. The Portuguese began signalling, but as Captain Walsh was below deck, no return was made. A shot across his bow brought the captain quickly up on deck and with the *Maria Crowther* hove to, the *San Josef* came closer for an inspection. A voice in English asked Captain Walsh if he had sighted any Spanish or Portuguese privateers, (pirate ships) sailing to South America where an attempt was underway to defeat the dominion of Spain and Portugal. Captain Walsh answered no.

As the huge ship came nearer towering above the little *Maria Crowther*, her passengers caught sight of evil-looking ragged sailors staring down at them. All aboard the *Maria Crowther* were concerned – captain, crew and passengers alike. Captain Walsh well understood the danger that they were in. Vessels were often boarded, plundered and burnt by the pirate ships that plagued the area. Luckily the captain of the *San Josef* soon lost interest in such a small prize and sailed away. That afternoon they were overhauled by another vessel, an English naval sloop. When her commander heard about the Portuguese vessels he put his ship about in pursuit.

As the *Maria Crowther* passed the Rock of Gibraltar they saw the Barbary Coast reflected in the sun's rays; Keats commented on the savage beauty of the scene and Severn made a sketch for a watercolour. Severn also noticed that Keats seemed calmer, with a look of serenity about his care-worn features. Severn made two sketches of Keats during the voyage – a pencil drawing of him in his bunk reading, and another, a watercolour of the poet sitting on a chair hunched over a book. The pencil drawing is lost, but the watercolour is now in the Keats Museum at Hampstead. In the portrait the nose looks unnaturally large on a thin pale face. His hair hangs loose, dark, lank and unwashed.

After a voyage of five weeks, in the early morning of the 21st of October, the *Maria Crowther* entered the Bay of Naples. After the damp dark cabin it was like a dream; the sparkling water, the brightly painted local boats. The view of the great harbour with the cone of the volcano Vesuvius, a plume of smoke tinted with gold in the sunlight as a backdrop. But their relief of having at last safely arrived soon turned to further disappointment; the harbour was crowded with ships. And as the *Maria Crowther* eased her way through the packed anchorage searching for a berth, the reason for the congestion was revealed. The harbour authorities in Naples, well versed in the danger of sickness from other countries being brought ashore, had heard about an outbreak of typhus fever in London. Ships from the Port of London were banned from landing merchandise or passengers until six weeks had elapsed from the beginning of their voyage; Keats and Severn had ten more days to serve trapped aboard the ship.

Severn was delighted by the sights and sounds, and although his view ashore was interrupted by a forest of ships' masts he sketched away. John tried to make the best of their situation. Miss Cotterell was desperately ill, but even she seemed happier now they were in port. Keats' medical background came into the fore, he began to regard her as almost his patient, and maybe her sufferings helped him quell his own. With Severn he conversed about the ancient Greeks, and their world which he had featured in his poems. The Greek Galleys and Tyrrhenian sloops trading with the mysterious East. Rowing boats filled with colourful people passed by the *Maria Crowther*, laughing and singing as they came alongside, bartering fresh fruit, grapes, figs, peaches and melons. This delighted the ship's passengers, especially Keats who had a fondness for fruit. Severn felt that they had arrived in paradise!

As for John, his spirits were raised, but he felt somehow apart from the lives of those around him. "Every man who can row his boat and walk and talk seems different from myself," he wrote to Mrs Brawne. From one of the passing boats someone hailed them in English, and when the boat came nearer they saw that it was crewed by English sailors. The officer in command, Lieutenant Sullivan was with the

British Squadron anchored in the bay. Sullivan and six sailors came aboard the *Maria Crowther*. Watching from the shore the port officials considered that the quarantine had been breached; the seven sailors must stay on board. Keats and Severn took a liking to the smart young officer immediately he stepped aboard, and the inconvenience of the seven extra bodies was eased by Lieutenant Sullivan's cheerfulness.

Keats managed to finish the letter to Mrs Brawne, he told her about the hardships of the voyage, the quarantine and how he had been affected by the other invalid aboard.

To Mrs Brawne.
                              Tuesday 24 Oct 1820.
Address: Mrs Brawne, Wentworth Place, Hampstead Middx, England.
Postmark F.P.O. 11 NO 1820.
                              Oct 24 Naples Harbour –
                                      care Giovanni.
My dear Mrs Brawne,
    A few words will tell you what sort of a Passage we had, and what situation we are in, and few they must be on account of the Quarantine, our Letters being liable to be opened for the purpose of fumigation at the Health Office. We have to remain in the vessel ten days and are, at present shut in a tier of ships. The air has been beneficial to me about to as great an extent as squally weather and bad accommodations and provisions has done harm – So I am about as I was – Give my Love to Fanny and tell her, if I were well there is enough in this Port of Naples to fill a quire of Paper – but it looks like a dream – every man who can row his boat and walk and talk seems a different being from myself. I do not feel in the world. It has been unfortunate for me that one of the Passengers is a young Lady in a Consumption – her imprudence has vexed me very much – the knowledge of her complaint

131

– the flushings in her face, all her bad symptoms have preyed upon me – they would have done so had I been in good health. Severn now is a very good fellow but his nerves are too strong to be hurt by other people's illnesses – I remember poor Rice wore me in the same way in the Isle of Wight – I shall feel a load off me when the Lady vanishes out of my sight. It is impossible to describe exactly in what state of health I am – at this moment I am suffering from indigestion very much, which makes such stuff of this Letter. I would always wish you to think me a little worse than I really am; not being of a sanguine disposition I am likely to succeed.

If I do not recover your regret will be softened if I do your pleasure will be doubled – I dare not fix my Mind upon Fanny, I have not dared to think of her. The only comfort I have had that way has been thinking for hours together of having the knife she gave me put in a silver-case – the hair in a Locket – and the Pocket Book in a gold net – Show her this. I dare say no more – Yet you must not believe I am so ill as this Letter may look, for if ever there was a person born without the faculty of hoping I am he. Severn is writing to Haslam, and I have just asked him to request Haslam to send you his account of my health. O'what an account I could give you of the Bay of Naples if I could once more feel myself a Citizen of this world – I feel a spirit in my Brain would lay it forth pleasantly – O what a misery it is to have an intellect in splints! My Love again to Fanny – tell Tootts I wish I could pitch her a basket of grapes – [Toots – Fanny's younger sister Margaret] – and tell Sam the fellows catch here with a line a little fish much like an anchovy, pull them up fast. [Sam Brawne, Fanny's brother the youngest member of the Brawne family]

Remember me to Mrs and Mr Dilke – mention to Brown that I wrote him a letter at Portsmouth which I did not send and am in doubt if he will ever see it.

my dear Mrs Brawne
Yours sincerely and affectionate
John Keats –
Good bye Fanny! God bless you

"Good bye Fanny! God bless you." It was his final message to her. On the 31st of October, Keats' birthday, the passengers were at last allowed to disembark. With the help of Charles Cotterell, the brother of the sick Miss Cotterell, a banker in Naples, Keats and Severn were soon settled into comfortable lodgings – a small trattoria with a view of the volcano, the Villa di Londra in the Vico S. Giuseppe, a narrow noisy street. The weather was now the opposite of Keats' image of the Italian climate, the skies were cloudy and a misty drizzle obscured the mountain.

On their first morning ashore they sat down and wrote letters to friends in England. Severn wrote to Haslam and Keats to Brown. Keats tried to write a short calm letter, but after two sentences he lost the will to write more; "I have gone thus far into it, I must go on a little; perhaps it may relieve the load of WRETCHEDNESS which presses upon me." The word WRETCHEDNESS in capitals seemed to express the depth of his misery.

Wednesday 1 Nov 1820.

To Charles Brown.

Naples, 1 Nov 1820.

My dear Brown,

Yesterday we were let out of Quarantine, during which my health suffered more from bad air and the stifled cabin than it had done the whole voyage. The fresh air revived me a little, and I hope I am well enough this morning to write to you a short calm letter; – if that can be called one, in which I am afraid to

133

speak of what I would fainest dwell upon. As I have gone thus far into it, I must go on a little; – perhaps it may relieve the load of WRETCHEDNESS which presses upon me. The persuasion that I shall see her no more will kill me. I cannot q – [he stopped the sentence here and could not continue with it, not finishing what was most likely the word QUIT] My dear Brown I should have had her when I was in health, and I should have remained well. [The mistaken idea of the time, that a love unconsummated brought ill health.] I can bear to die – I cannot bear to leave her.

O,God! God! God! Everything I have in my trunks that reminds me of her goes through me like a spear. The silk lining she put in my travelling cap scalds my head. My imagination is horribly vivid about her – I see her – I hear her. There is nothing in the world of sufficient interest to divert me from her a moment. This was the case when I was in England; I cannot recollect, without shuddering, the time that I was a prisoner at Hunt's, and used to keep my eyes fixed on Hampstead all day. Then there was a good hope of seeing her again – Now! – O'that I could be buried near where she lives!

I am afraid to write to her – to receive a letter from her – to see her hand writing would break my heart – even to hear of her anyhow, to see her name written, would be more than I could bear. My dear Brown, What am I to do? Where can I look for consolation or ease? If I had any chance of recovery, this passion would kill me. Indeed, through the whole of my illness, both at your house and at Kentish Town, this fever never ceased wearing me out. When you write to me, which you will do immediately, write to Rome (poste restante) – if she is well and happy, put a mark thus +; if –

Remember me to all. I will endeavour to bear my miseries patiently. A person in my state of health should not have such miseries to bear. Write a short note to my sister, saying you have heard from me. Severn is very well. If I were in better health I would urge your coming to Rome. I fear there is no one can give me any comfort. Is there any news of George? O' that something fortunate had ever happened to me or my brothers! – then I might hope, – but despair is forced upon me as a habit. My dear Brown, for my sake, be her advocate forever. I cannot say a word about Naples; I do not feel at all concerned in the thousand novelties around me. I am afraid to write to her – I should like her to know that I do not forget her. Oh, Brown, I have coals of fire in my breast. It surprises me that the human heart is capable of containing and bearing so much misery. Was I born for this end? God bless her, and her mother, and my sister, and George, and his wife, and you, and all!

Your ever affectionate friend,
John Keats

He was too early for the post and added to his letter a postscript:

Thursday 2 November. – I was a day too early for the Courier. He sets out now. I have been more calm today, though in a half dread of not continuing so. I said nothing of my health; I know nothing of it; you will hear Severn's account from Haslam. I must leave off. You bring my thoughts too near to Fanny. God bless you! [Ends]

The letter that was written on board the *Maria Crowther* and addressed to Mrs Brawne, is on paper stained and discoloured, probably from the effects of decontamination by the Naples Office of Health.

We can guess at the state of Keats' mind by reading these letters. He is now in pain and despair, nothing can lift him, from now on he is overwhelmed.

John's suffering began to communicate itself to Severn. Keats had before complained that Severn's nerves were too strong. Severn's natural light-hearted disposition had up to now protected him, but now that the state his friend was in was plain to see he was deeply affected. One morning he hurried from the room bursting into uncontrollable tears. Somehow he believed that he had hidden this weakness from Keats. However the poet had noticed the change, and realised that Severn was beginning to be troubled by their situation. After dinner that same night, John took his friend to one side saying that he wished to talk. What he said is uncertain, for Severn never revealed the content of the conversation. Except to say that it was "Much, very much; I don't know whether it was the more painful for me or himself, but I was very affected by what he disclosed, which brought yet again tears to my eyes."

Charles Cotterell, the banker, warned them not to expect too much of Naples. And they soon realised the truth behind his warning for themselves. The weather improved as the rain eased, and they were able to venture out onto the narrow streets. Severn gave a vivid description of the surroundings:

"Everything seemed offensive, except the glorious autumnal atmosphere, and the sense of light and joy of the vintage, which was everywhere in evidence. With songs and laughter and cries, and endless coming and going, the whole city seemed in motion. The city itself, with its indiscriminate noises and bewildering smells, struck us as one great kitchen, for cooking was going on in every street, and at almost every house; at, not in, for it was all done out-of-doors or upon the thresholds. At every corner was a bare-legged Neapolitan devouring macaroni and roaring for more; mariners in red caps were hawking fish at the tip-top of their voices; and everywhere beggars were strumming guitars or howling ballads. The whole occupation of the citizens seemed to be done in the streets, and never ceased, for, as we soon experienced, it went on all night, so that at first we could not sleep for the continued row."

They stayed in Naples for four days. Charles Cotterell and a few members of the English colony were kind and attentive. They drove out of the city into the countryside; Keats was delighted by the colours and abundant flowers. During these rides his good humour returned. One morning he was delighted by the sight of road menders sitting by the wayside eating macaroni; "who scorned the humbug of knives and forks." There was excitement amongst the crowds about the streets. Revolution was in the air! The rule of Austria had for a time been broken, and the soldiers of the King were everywhere. They were a dangerous half-starved and undisciplined looking band. The Neapolitans had suffered from years of poverty, the streets were full of beggars badgering passers-by – hardly the environment for one such as Keats, sick as he was in mind and body. But still, taking all into account Severn wanted stay at Naples. He believed that the kindness of Cotterell and his friends might prove to be better for Keats than the unknown conditions he might find in Rome. Keats however felt anxious there, and wished to get away. Two days after the liberation, the King of Naples betrayed his supporters to the Austrians and deserted the city.

One evening the two friends went to the theatre, The San-Carlo, the interior of which was so heavily gilded that Severn remarked that it seemed to be built entirely of gold. As with most theatres at the time the stench was overpowering. The play production was poor, but Keats liked the style of the scene paintings. There were soldiers about the theatre, even on each side of the stage. At first John thought that they were part of the production, and was disturbed to learn that in fact this was not so. The sentries were there to oversee and control the audience. John was outraged. He said, "that he could not bear to think that he might die and be buried in such a place as Naples was; and declared that he would at once leave for Rome." The next day a letter arrived from Shelley, extending a further invitation to stay with him, and offering advice on how to live in Italy.

Arrangements had already been made with a Dr Clark in Rome to find suitable accommodation for the travellers. The poet was to be his patient. The letter of credit was in place with Torlonia the Rome banker, it was time to make a move.

Charles Cotterell gave an informal farewell dinner for them, and the next morning they set out in a small carriage drawn by a slow ancient horse. Severn was easily able to walk alongside as they crawled along. It was a beautiful day and he enjoyed the air and exercise. Keats, though he tried to match his friend's high spirits, felt tired and listless. They made their way through rich valleys, the hillsides covered with vineyards, with grape vines hanging, curving in lines from post to post. Severn, although he kept his thoughts to himself, felt that the land was wasted on the Italians, who he considered a lazy idle collection of men! The inns they stopped at were particularly bad. The food was of poor quality, the accommodation uncomfortable. At last they arrived at the Roman Campagna; a vast uneven wasteland that Keats likened to an inland sea. The scenery was desolate and menacing, an area said to be frequented by bands of robbers.

At one place on the road they saw a dot of bright red in the distance. As they came near it turned into the scarlet cloak of a Catholic cardinal. He was occupied in shooting small wild duck, which he attracted toward him using a mirror fixed to a stick. His carriage stood at the roadside attended by two servants, who were loading his fowling pieces. Keats commented on the number of dead birds in a pile near the carriage.

The journey to Rome must have taken nine weary days. For it was the 15th of November when at last they came upon the old Aurelian wall of the city rising before them. On the last stretch of the Appian Way they found posts, on which hung the bodies of bandits and criminals who had been taken out beyond the city walls for execution. Keats turned aside, shocked at the barbarity of the age in which he lived. In England public executions still took place, and the prisons were terrible places. (It would be 1842 before reform, and the building of Pentonville Prison, which was considered at the time a model of progress.)

They had no trouble from the officials checking visas at the gate. The documents they had collected from the British Legation in Naples were in order. As the carriage slowly made its way through the Lateran Gate, the vast ruin of the Coliseum dominated the skyline. Keats remarked on its terrible history as they gazed in awe at its majesty. Severn requested the carriage driver to take them onto The Piazza di Spagna, at the time the centre of the English colony.

Dr James Clark sat in his room at the time of their arrival, he was about to write a letter to Naples enquiring as to the whereabouts of his patient. From his window he watched the slow approach of the conveyance, and went down to meet the weary travellers. He was immediately impressed by Keats, though initially thought Severn not the best companion for a sick man. He had already booked rooms for them on the opposite side of the piazza, beside the famous wide stone steps leading up to the Church of the Trinita dei Monti (The Spanish Steps) so-called because the Spanish Consulate building was situated in the square. There were so many English in the city at that time that the word traveller was synonymous with Englishman. The English above all others were considered rich, and this was reflected in the amount that the Italians charged them for accommodation. Many of the foreigners were on what was termed the 'Grand Tour'. Other British lived there, they were professionals or in

139

business; doctors, bankers, shop and innkeepers. The rooms that Dr Clark had reserved for Keats and Severn were in number 26, Piazza di Spagna, at the foot of the Spanish Steps. The rent was to be £5 a month for the rooms, with food and services extra. In an apartment below, an Englishman, Thomas Gibson lived with his valet. On the floors above Keats and Severn the two apartments were occupied – one by a James O'Hara with his servant, and in the other an Italian army officer and his wife. The only disadvantage for Keats and Severn was the closeness of the landlady. Anna Angeletti, a middle-aged Venetian lived just across the hallway. When she realised that one of her new lodgers was ill she argued with Dr Clark about accepting them. The authorities in Rome at the time were very strict about infection control. Dr Clark managed to persuade her that he would be responsible for any problems that might arise, and she reluctantly agreed that they could stay. Keats realised that they would be continually under her observation and felt that they were to be spied upon.

The main part of the apartment consisted of a bright sitting room, about fifteen feet square; leading off of this, there was a double-windowed room just eight feet wide which led into a small room that overlooked the steps. Severn set up his painting equipment in the smallest room. Keats took the room overlooking the Piazza below for himself and Severn made up a bed in the sitting room. John urged Severn to begin work on the picture he was to submit to the Academy; the subject for this new picture 'The Death of Alcibiades'. However Severn worried that the morbid nature of the subject might affect Keats and he worked on it secretly. While his friend worked, Keats picked up his study of Italian, even thinking about writing a long poem based on Milton's Sabrina. He endeavoured to keep cheerful for Severn's sake, but in his mind he knew that he was to unwell to compose or write anything. Dr Clark came every day, he made every effort to ease his patient's mind from whatever troubled him so much. Severn by this time knew what it was that so distressed his friend.

On the 30th of November Keats wrote his last letter, a letter to a man to whom he believed he was greatly indebted.

To Charles Brown.

Rome, 30 November 1820.

[No address or postmark]

My dear Brown,
'Tis the most difficult thing in the world to me to write a letter. My stomach continues so bad, that I feel it worse on opening any book, – yet I am much better than I was in quarantine. Then I am afraid to encounter the pro-ing and con-ing of anything interesting to me in England. I have an habitual feeling of my real life having passed, and that I am leading a posthumous existence. God knows how it would have been – but it appears to me – however, I will not speak of that subject. I must have been at Bedhampton nearly at the time you were writing to me from Chichester – how unfortunate – and to pass on the river too! There was my star predominate! [*All's Well That Ends Well*, Shakespeare] – I cannot answer anything in your letter, which followed me from Naples to Rome, because I am afraid to look it over again. I am so weak (in mind) that I cannot bear the sight of any handwriting of a friend I love so much as I do you. Yet I ride the little horse, [Dr Clark had hired a pony for Keats to ride, thinking to get his patient out more. In the rate of exchange at the time the cost of the horse was £6 a month. Keats very soon gave up the riding] and, at my worst, even in quarantine, summoned up more puns, [jokes off the cuff on the happenings of a moment] in a sort of desperation in one week than in any year of my life. There is one thought enough to kill me; I have been well, healthy, alert, &c., walking with her, and

141

know – the knowledge of contrast, feeling for the light and shade, all that information (primitive sense) necessary for a poem, are great enemies to the recovery of the stomach. There you rogue, I put you to the torture; but you must bring your philosophy to bear, as I do mine, really, or how should I be able to live? Dr Clark is very attentive to me; he says there is very little the matter with my lungs, but my stomach he says, is very bad. I am well disappointed in hearing good news from George, for it runs in my head we shall all die young. I have not written to Reynolds yet, which he must think me very neglectful; being anxious to send him a good account of my health, I have delayed it from week to week. If I recover, I will do all in my power to correct the mistakes made during sickness; and if not all my faults will be forgiven. Severn is very well, though he leads so dull a life with me. Remember me to all friends, and tell Haslam I should not have left London without asking leave of him, but being so low in body and mind. Write to George as soon as you receive this, and tell him how I am, as far as you can guess; and also a note to my sister – who walks about my imagination like a ghost – she is so like Tom. I can scarcely bid you good-bye, even in a letter. I always made an awkward bow.

God bless you!

John Keats.

This as far as we know was the very last letter that Keats wrote. He received other letters whilst in Italy, both from Charles Brown and Fanny Brawne, but refused to open or read them.

We have part of a letter from George in America, that is written in answer to one that Brown sent him at Keats' request. This letter is catalogued as being in answer to one from Joseph Severn, but as it carries no name or address we can only surmise, however it is likely to be to Brown.

George writes that the letter he received had a coldness about it, it's unlikely that Severn would have written in such a vein, but we know that Brown was harbouring a hatred for George. He sat planning vengeance for the way George had, or so he believed stolen away the last of Keats' inheritance. He wrote; "exposure and infamy shall consign him to perpetual exile. I will have no mercy, the world will cry aloud for the cause of Keats' untimely death, and I will give it."

George wrote from Louisville on the 3rd of March 1821:

Sir,

I am obliged for yours of the Dec 21st informing me that my Brother is in Rome, and that he is better. The coldness of your letter explains itself; I hope John is not impressed with the same sentiments, it may be an amiable resentment on your part and you are at liberty to cherish it; whatever errors you may fall into thro' kindness to my Brother however injurious to me, are easily forgiven. I might have reasonably hoped a longer siege of doubts would be necessary to destroy your good opinion of me. In many letters of distant and late dates to John, to you and to Haslam unanswered, I have explained my prospects, my situation. I have a firm faith that John has every dependence on my honour and affection, and altho' the chances have gone against me, my disappointments having been just as numerous as my risques.

I am still above water and hope soon to be able to relieve him. I once more thank you most fervently for your kindness to John. and am Sir

Your Obt Hbl serv
George Keats.

Letters passed to and fro across seas and oceans, the information within them stale and out of date before coming before the eyes of those intended to read them. Brown's last letter to Keats was dated December 1820.

From Charles Brown. Hampstead.

Thursday 21 Dec 1820

To John Keats Esq. Poste Restante. Rome. en Italie.

My Dear Keats,

Not two hours since your letter from Rome 30th Nov came to me – and as to-morrow is post night, you shall have the answer in due course. And so you still wish me to follow you to Rome? and truly I wish to go – nothing detains me but prudence. Little could be gained, if anything, by letting my house at this time of year, and the consequences would be a heavy additional expense which I cannot possibly afford, – unless it were a matter of necessity, and I see none while you are in such good hands as Severn's. As for my appropriating any part of remittances from George, that is out of the question while you continue disabled from writing. Thank God you are getting better! Your last letter which I so gravely answered about 4th Dec showed how much you had suffered by the voyage & the cursed quarantine. Keep your mind easy, my dear fellow, & no fear of your body. Your sister I hear is in remarkably good health, The last news from George (already given to you) was so far favourable that there were no complaints. Every body next door is quite well.

Taylor has just returned to Town, – I saw him for a few minutes the other day, & had not time to put some questions which I wished, – but I understand your poems increase in sale. Hunt has been very ill, but is now recovered. All other friends are well. I know you don't like John Scott, [Scott, magazine editor and a contributor to the *Morning Chronicle*] but he is doing a thing that tickles me to the heart's core, and you will like to hear of it, if you have any revenge in your composition. By some means 'crooked enough I dare say' he has got possession of one of Blackwood's gang, who has turned King's evidence, [Blackwood's; the paper that had labelled Keats a member of the Cockney School, rubbishing Endymion and his other poems] and month after month he belabours them with the most damning facts that can be conceived; – if they are indeed facts, I know not how the rogues can stand against them. This virulent attack has made me like the London Magazine, [John Scott's Magazine] & I sent the 1st chapter of my Tour for Scott to publish, if he would pay me 10 Gns per sheet, & print the whole chapters monthly, without my forfeiting the copyright in the end. This would have answered my purpose famously, – but he won't agree to my stipulations. He praises my writing wondrously, – will pay the 10 Gns & so on, – but the fellow forsooth must have the chapters somewhat converted into the usual style on magazine articles, & so the treaty is at an end. O, – I must tell you Abby is living with me again, but not in the same capacity – she keeps to her own bed, & I keep myself continent. Any more nonsense of the former kind would put me in an awkward predicament with her. One child is very well. She behaves extremely well, and, by what I hear from Sam, [Samuel Brawne, Fanny Brawne's young brother living next door] my arrangements prevents the affair from giving pain next door. The fact is I could not afford to allow her a separate establishment. Mrs Brawne at first 'I thought' behaved tolerably well, – I can't say so much for her now; – her husband knows nothing of the matter yet, as she says. [this is the first mention of Fanny's father, and seems strange as Fanny's father was deceased. It looks as if Mrs Brawne was beginning to give Brown a hard time about his living arrangements!] In the meantime the child thrives gloriously, but I'm not going to be fondly parental, for, between you & me, I think an infant is a disagreeable, – it is all gut and squall. I dined with Richards on his wedding day, – [Charles Richards, the Printer] he had just recovered from breaking his leg, – how could he be so brittle? – and it was done in a game of romps with his children! – Now I've something to make you 'spit fire, spout flame', the batch of Brag players asked me to town, hoping to fleece me, – it was at Reynold's lodging, – & I carried off £2.10/, – when will they be sick of these vain attempts? Mrs Dilke was next door yesterday, – she had a sad tumble in the mud, – 'you must not laugh'- her news was that Martin is to be married this year, – that Reynolds & Mrs Montague correspond sentimentally, – & that Barry Cornwall is to have Miss Montague, – [Barry Cornwall, song lyric, and poetry writer] – there's some interesting small talk for you. Oh! Barry C: has a tragedy coming forth at the Theatre, – christened Mirandola, – Mire and O la! – What an odd being you are, – because you & I were so near meeting twice, yet missed each other both times, you cry out "there was my star predominant!" – why not mine 'CB's' as well? But this is the way you argue yourself into fits of spleen. If I were in Severn's place, & you insisted on ever gnawing a bone, I'd lead you the life of a dog. What the devil should you grumble for? Do you recollect my anagram on your name?- how pat it comes now to Severn! – my love to him & the said anagram. "Thanks Joe" if I have a right guess, a certain person next door is a little disappointed at not receiving a letter from you, but not a word has dropped. She wrote to you lately, and so did your sister.

Yours most faithfully,
Cha's Brown.

Brown's letters and those from his sister and Fanny Brawne lay unopened in the poet's sick room. Dying, he requested Severn to inter them with him in his coffin, and he did so.

Although by this time Dr Clark had taken his patient off the starvation diet, Keats had little interest in food. When in his old age Severn had told a visitor that Keats' stomach trouble had not been improved by the fare sent up from the little restaurant (Trattoria) situated below on the ground floor of the house. He seemed to believe that it belonged to Anna Angeletti their landlady. Keats' complaints about the food were of no avail. Finally he said, "If she will not listen I have a plan to mend the matter." He refused to reveal to Severn exactly what his plan entailed. When next the waiter came up with their food, John looked at it, turned up his nose and smiled at Severn. Then taking the box from the man he went over to the open window and dropped the box, food, and crockery, all down to the square below. Shouts and laughter came up from below in which the two friends and the waiter joined. "Now," said John, "we shall maybe get a decent dinner." Shortly afterwards the still-smiling servant delivered a better meal. From that time on the food was very much improved, but they found that they were being charged extra for it!

After a few days, and when they had settled in, Keats asked Dr Clark if it would be possible to have some music. Severn could play the piano; the landlady had one in her sitting room and Clark persuaded her to have it moved over to the sitting room of her lodgers. Dr Clark's wife sent over some sheet music, which included the Haydn symphonies. Severn was from then on able to amuse Keats with his playing. John especially liked the Haydn, "This Haydn is like a child, for there is no knowing what he will do next!"

Soon after their arrival in Rome, Keats insisted that Severn should take the opportunity to further his own career. Severn had letters brought from England, introductions to other artists, and now Dr Clark arranged for him a meeting with John Gibson the sculptor. The meeting was to take place at Gibson's studio, and when Severn arrived the connoisseur and patron of the arts Lord Colchester was already there.

Severn apologised and made to go, but Gibson insisted that he should come in, and offered him the same courtesy as his rich patron. Severn said, "This made him feel that artists must be of more consequence in Italy than they were in England."

Keats had not been sure that coming to Italy would be of any advantage to his friend and his career, or help with his application to the Academy for the scholarship, for here was an artist applying for the Rome Scholarship when he was already there. He had another reason for thinking that there might be opposition to the award and pension. He told Severn that a group of painters around the Academy were, he knew, full of jealousy. Keats had been at a dinner when Severn's previous Gold Medal award was being discussed. One member of the party had said that it had been given to an old man, who had tried for it so many times that the Council had taken pity on him. Keats waited for someone to speak in Severn's defence. One, Hilton, who knew Severn personally sat impassive at the table, and the insult was not withdrawn. Keats rose from his chair, "He would no longer sit at table with such traducers and snobs; they very well knew that Severn was a young man, and had never before tried for an award of any kind. He knew him well, and had seen and admired the picture at first hand." With that outburst he left the room and stormed out of De-Wint's house (Peter De-Wint, 1784–1849, landscape painter). Severn was surprised by the news, but realised that what had taken place was perhaps more about Keats than himself.

As John began to get acclimatised, the timeless city of Rome calmed his troubled spirit. For a time he felt better and was able to ascend the Spanish Steps up to the Pincio. There, sitting under the ilex (holly) trees, he had a view over the city, in the middle distance the dome of St Peter's, a dark purple illuminated by winter sunshine. Out on his walks he met and became friendly with a Lieutenant Eton, another consumptive. The two men strolled the tree-lined walkways together, and one day visited the Villa Borghese where they saw the semi-nude statue of Pauline Buonaparte, a new work by Canova. Keats thought the statue vulgar, and likened it to an 'Aeolian Harp' "because every wind could play upon it."

"His not right feelings toward women" affected him still! Out one day walking on the Pincio, they met the model herself: she stared so hard at Elton who was smart and good-looking, that Keats felt uncomfortable, and declared, "He would walk on the Pincian Hill no longer."

There were other attractions close by their lodgings. Going out from the Piazza past the goldsmiths and the Torlonia Bank, then down to the Corso the main area of thriving commercial life in the city.

Keats had been lucky in a way that John Taylor his publisher had found Dr James Clark, he was a well-read 32-year-old. His qualifications were as good as any at the time, he had a good bedside manner and was cautious in his diagnoses. A believer in good diet and fresh air. He had written a paper on the beneficial effects of the Italian climate on those suffering with ailments of the lungs. Having observed Keats carefully, he noted that his patient was suffering badly from stomach pain – the tuberculosis had reached his stomach. He seemed to think that there was little wrong with Keats' lungs; how wrong he was to be proved!

On the tenth of December the period of remission ended. Severn had been out for his morning walk, and when he returned mid-morning he found Keats soaked with perspiration asleep in his bed. Later when mixing his paints to begin work he heard a cry from Keats' bedroom. On going to him, he was shocked to find the sheet and bed covers covered in blood. He immediately summoned Dr Clark, who found his patient sweating and in a high fever. As was always the practice at the time, Clark bled him, taking a full eight ounces from his left arm. Keats stared up at Severn with a strange brightness in his eyes; then in an anguished voice exclaimed; "this day shall be my last." He pleaded with his friend to bring him the bottle of laudanum. Severn, guessing why he wanted it, refused. Keats raged on at him in his delirium, but Severn remained firm.

Later on he calmed down, but still in a steady voice pleaded for help to end his life. "My dear friend, this will spare you the anguish of watching my squalid slow death!" Severn returned gently but firmly, saying "That to end his life in that manner would be wrong. His friends all sincerely wished for a recovery, and that for himself he felt it a privilege to be allowed to care for him." Dr Clark came, and Severn warned him about his patient's state of mind, passing him the laudanum for safekeeping.

As for Severn, we can pity him for the predicament that he found himself in. And admire his strength of character for the way that he handled a difficult situation. He was alone in strange land, trapped within a terrible situation. As a confirmed Christian, Severn's convictions forbade him to allow a suicide. Over the period of the following nine days Keats suffered five more haemorrhages. With his staring eyes he horrified Severn into believing that his mind was now permanently damaged. Dr Clark, despairing, watched closely, and tried another starvation diet. His wife searched the city for the best fish, which she prepared and cooked herself. It made little difference, for by now his stomach was so bad that nothing stayed within him. The attacks of diarrhoea continued and he raved that that he would die of starvation.

Clark held out little hope of recovery. He told Severn, "I have nothing to treat a diseased mind." He wrote to John Taylor in England, saying that Keats was "in a most deplorable state, the stomach is ruined and the state of his mind is the worst possible for one in his condition. And will undoubtedly hurry on an event that I fear is not far distant." Joseph Severn was now on his own. For fear of contracting the illness, neither the landlady or any of the servants came near. He was making the beds, changing the soiled sheets, fetching their food and drink, reading to the invalid and attending to his incessant demands. The other people living within the house, the tenants below and above, each with their own servants seem not to have lifted a finger. William Ewing, a sculptor living near by came to visit, relieving the hard-pressed Severn for a few hours.

After the relapse in December, Severn wrote unhappy letters to the waiting friends in England. It was from Brown that Mrs Brawne and Fanny heard on the seventeenth of January the distressing news. Just the day before Fanny had written to the poet's sister, cheerfully telling Fanny Keats of her brother riding the little horse in Rome. In Rome, Christmas came, with Joseph Severn recalling later that it was the saddest that he had ever spent. The fever having eased, Keats got up and sat in the sitting room. This was kept from the landlady, for Anna Angeletti had reported to the city authorities that she had a dying man in her rooms. This meant that by Rome's laws at the time that everything within the rooms would have to be burnt. Compensation had to be made by the tenants to the owners of the property. In the sitting room alone there were furnishings with an estimated value of a hundred and fifty pounds. It was going to be difficult to even cover the cost of the furniture in the small bedroom. Severn had no money of his own, and he knew that nothing would be left over from the funds that their friends had sent from England. Whilst Keats was in the sitting room the door leading to the landlady's apartment was blocked off.

Severn's heart was younger than his years, he was apt to look at life through rose-tinted spectacles. Keats must have worried as to what the future had in store for his young artist friend. "Severn," he said, "I bequeath to you all the happiness I have ever known." Now a little embarrassed, and thinking that Keats' mind was wandering again, Severn raised his hand in a gesture of acknowledgement. But Keats carried on, his voice steady, "This is the last Christmas I shall ever see, but I hope you will see many and be happy. It would be a second death for me, if I knew that your goodness now was your loss hereafter."

If only he had known that what he considered to be Severn's sacrifice would be the means of ensuring the painter's future prosperity. For it was his devotion to Keats in those desperate hours of need that secured his reputation, firstly amongst the English living in Italy and then spreading far and wide with patrons throughout Europe.

And now to add to his worries the problem of money arose. On their arrival they had drawn on the letter of credit at the Torlonia Bank the sum of £120, this left just £30 of the original £150 deposited. Taylor had expected small amounts to be drawn as required. The bank informed Dr Clark that withdrawals made in this way would attract handling charges. Being in ignorance of the bank's handling of the account, when Taylor and Hessey received a charge for the £120 they believed that Keats and Severn were living beyond their means and stopped further payments. When Severn found the £30 balance denied him he panicked. How were they to manage? He kept the news from Keats and went to Clark for help. The doctor agreed to explain the situation to the publishers in England, and granted Severn a loan from his own account. Taylor wrote to Torlonia requesting resumption of payment, and set about a further collection of funds in England. He soon received donations of £10 each from five of Keats' friends. Richard Woodhouse, Taylor and Hessey's reader and lawyer put in £50 himself. Another £50 came from Taylor's friend and patron of the arts Earl Fitzwilliam. They all hoped that George's promise of money from America would one day materialise. It's very probable that these extra funds did arrive, for later all of the debts in Italy were finally settled. However it would be the end of February before Severn's money worries came to an end, and by then Keats had died.

In the middle of the January he had rallied for a short time, and on two occasions had even felt strong enough to venture out onto the piazza. The square bustled with flower sellers and by the Barcaccia Fountain people in period costume gathered, waiting to be hired as models for the many artists in the city. The respite however was brief, and he was soon back in bed almost to weak to raise himself up.

After Christmas letters arrived from England, one each from Charles Brown, the publisher Hessey and Fanny Brawne. He could not bear to read them, handing them to Severn unopened.

Fanny's letter was never to be opened! If he had read it, he would have known of her disappointment at not getting a letter from him, for he had failed to write a single word directly to her since leaving England. Seeing her handwriting on the envelope set him off again on the strange topic of unfulfilled love – that he had been denied sexual satisfaction and that this was the cause of his illness! Severn listened to many things that he would gloss over in later years. He wrote to Brown in February, saying how Keats "found many causes of his illness in the thwarting of his passions, but I persuaded him to feel otherwise on this delicate point."

As Keats went in the final stage of his illness he would not let Severn out of his sight. John rejected any thought of an existence after death. "Death is the great divorcer for ever, I die without the spiritual comforts that any common rogue or fool has in his last moments." Years afterward Severn would persuade himself that Keats had prayed near the end. However there is no evidence that he accepted any comfort from his friends Christianity. He intimated that death would be his only comfort. By the first week of February Severn realised that Keats was dying, he had looked almost without hope for a miracle recovery, but now even that hopeless of hopes disappeared. John's weakness desperate, during the night he was soaked with sweat, struggling to breathe, choking on the blood coming from his shattered lungs.

153

Severn sat by him both day and night. He set up a string of candles, so that as one extinguished it lit the next. One night John woke just as a candle was guttering, when suddenly another one lit up as if by magic. He exclaimed; "Severn, Severn! here's a little fairy lamplighter actually lit another candle."

Dr Clark noticed the strain that Severn was under. And afraid that he might break down, arranged for an English nurse to come in to relieve him. Keats took to her, and Severn was able to get out into the fresh air. He returned refreshed, to brighten John with tales of the activity out in the square. He told of seeing the first roses coming into bloom. But this was too much for the invalid and he burst into a flood of tears. He asked his friend to visit the site of what would be his last resting place –the cemetery for non-Catholics at the foot of Monte Testaccio, outside of the Aurelian Wall, and under the Pyramid of Caius Cestius. The ground at the time was covered in white daisies and blue violets were coming into bloom over the graves. A few ilex trees gave shade and the ancient tomb, the Pyramid of Caius Cestius pointed skywards, a reminder of times long past.

When Severn described the scene, Keats said, "I can already feel the flowers growing over me." Now that he had a picture in his mind of his last resting place, John began to set down what he wanted done. Severn broke down during the conversation, putting his head in his hands; Keats continued, "please don't distress yourself so, my dear Severn." He had accepted his fate and was now completely calm. He asked that Fanny Brawne's unopened letters should be placed within the coffin, together with a curl of her hair.

The purse that his sister had made and the hand cooling 'cornelian-stone' that even now he moved from one fevered hand to the other, and never in his last days put down; this stone that Fanny Brawne had used on hot summer days to cool her hands when at her dressmaking. This very personal object that she had owned since a young girl, and had placed in her lover's hand as they waited for the coach that would remove him from Hampstead, and her side, for ever. "Severn, make sure that this stone is placed in my hand as I am laid in my coffin." It seemed, thought Severn, "his only consolation, the only thing left him in this world clearly tangible." (From a letter from Severn to H.B. Forman.)

As the end drew near, the English nurse became ill; or at least she failed to turn up for duty. Maybe it was a fear of contracting consumption that kept her from the dying man's bedside. It was left to Severn to rise up for the final challenge. Somehow he found the will power to continue his ministry until the end.

Four days before he died, Keats went into a period of unusual calm. Severn felt that even now there might be the slightest chance of a miracle recovery, a drowning man – he clutched an unlikely straw!

John requested there be no obituary notices in the London newspapers, and that his gravestone should bear the simple inscription; "Here lies one whose name was writ in water." (Charles Armitage-Brown claimed that Keats had joked about this at a much earlier time.) Where it came from we can only guess at. Was it perhaps a quotation from another writer? Or did he feel himself so unimportant to the world that his name should remain invisible. This calm was remarkable after the passion and rages that had gone before. He had the mind of a genius, and a passionate nature, always going to extremes even as a young boy. During his suffering he had laid out his feelings for all to see. Now near death, his poet's view of life at last brought consolation. However he still rejected Severn's plea that Christ could save him. At this time his thoughts were almost all on Severn; "Did you ever see anyone die? Well I pity you, poor Severn."

During this time he lay for hours as if sleeping, when his eyes opened they had a confused look, until he saw Severn nearby looking down at him in consternation. The eyes still had that special light, a light that reminded Severn of the hours spent in the poet's company, hours that had brought both painter and poet so much pleasure.

On Friday the 23rd of February, Dr Clark brought the nurse back, enabling Severn to snatch a few hours' sleep. At four thirty in the afternoon Keats woke; the nurse shook the sleeping Severn awake, "He calls for you."

Keats whispered, "Severn, lift me up, for I am dying. I shall die easy." Looking into his friend's face he added, "Don't be frightened, thank God it has come." Severn held him as he fought for breath, a terrible sweat came over him, as he said, "Severn, don't take my breath, and don't breathe on me, your breath comes like ice." For seven more hours he struggled for breath, at times gripping Severn's hand. At eleven o'clock his breathing suddenly eased, the hand released its grip, a last rasp of phlegm rattled in his throat and he was dead.

His face looked relaxed and peaceful, he might have been just sleeping. Severn was at the point of collapse. And it was Dr Clark who took charge as he and the nurse prepared the body. To Severn he said, "We must pack and remove all his and your personal possessions before we notify the authorities, else they will be lost to you." On Saturday the 24th the papers were signed and a death certificate issued. Clark wrote, cause of death: 'Disease of the chest and stomach'. He arranged for a mask-maker to take casts of Keats' face, one hand and a foot. In the death mask the poet's facial features and cheekbones are shown in sharp relief, the nose is thin and sharp, the eye sockets sunken. These same features are visible in the pencil drawing that Severn did as Keats lay on his deathbed.

An autopsy performed by Clark and a Dr Luby revealed the lungs completely destroyed; Clark pronounced it the worst case of consumption he had ever seen. He told Severn, "I can't believe that he lasted for so long."

As darkness fell on the evening of the 25th, the coffin was brought to the apartment and placed on trestles in the sitting room. Keats' body dressed in his favourite jacket, and his white shirt with the high collar, was gently placed inside. The relics he had requested, the pocket book, penknife, and travelling cap, the last gifts from Fanny Brawne were laid at his side. The white cornelian stone that he had held to the last, was placed in his right hand. The unopened letters from his sister and Fanny as he had requested were also put in. Fanny Brawne's letter, Severn placed in the jacket breast pocket, over the poet's heart.

Anna Angeletti had been informed of the death, and her piano taken back to her apartment, saving it from destruction by the health office fumigators. The rules of burial in Rome at the time meant that funerals of non-Catholics were required to take place during the hours of darkness, at the Protestant Cemetery outside of the city walls. Dr Clark had agreed a dispensation with the authorities for the funeral to be conducted just before dawn. It was still dark on Monday the 26th when the carriage containing the coffin made its way through sleeping streets to the cemetery. Another carriage following close behind, brought the English Chaplain Dr Wolff who would conduct the service, and Joseph Severn with two young architects, Henry Parke and Ambrose Poynter who had befriended Keats and Severn. At the cemetery they were joined by Doctors Clark and Juby. Also in attendance were William Ewing, and Richard Westmacott, both sculptors.

In the records of the Protestant Cemetery, Keats' burial is recorded as taking place before daybreak in the morning. By the time the service was over it was nine o'clock and daylight. That he was buried at dawn seems certain. It was found recorded in a letter amongst papers given to the Keats – Shelley Memorial House by Sir Sidney Colvin. The letter in question was written about 1850 by Ambrose Poynter to his father, Sir E.J. Poynter R.A. – Ambrose Poynter attended at Keats' funeral. There was no address or postmark with the letter.

"There is much being said just now about Keats the poet, and some permanent memorial to be raised to him in the English Cemetery at Rome. This calls to mind that I went to his funeral there in 1821. The party consisted of his friend Severn who accompanied him to Italy and never left him to the last, Henry Parke, the Architect, the English Chaplain and myself (Ambrose Poynter, Architect). We started before daylight, a necessary precaution on a Protestant demonstration, we four in one carriage and the COFFIN in another, and arrived just before daybreak at the foot of the Pyramid of Caius Cestius."

Copied by H.M.Poynter. (Oct: 24th, 1821.)

Severn, exhausted and grief stricken, had to be supported by William Ewing as the coffin was lowered into the ground. It was Dr Clark, remembering a conversation with Keats towards the end, who asked the gravediggers to cover the earth with turfs of daisies.

Severn was shocked on returning to the rooms he had shared with Keats for almost three months, to find police and workmen removing the furniture for burning. Two men were already stripping paper from the walls, whilst another prepared the fumigation. The landlady had put some broken crockery on a small table; telling Severn that the breakages would be listed on the compensation bill. Severn, angry and hurt, relieved his feelings by finishing the breaking with his stick. Anna Angeletti apologised, but pointed out that the crockery had been broken when Keats had emptied the food and dishes from the window. Dr Clark smoothed the argument, promising that all compensation would be paid in full.

A month later, the extra funds from the collections in England were guaranteed with a letter of credit to the banker,

Torlonia, and a full settlement was made with the long-suffering landlady. Dr Clark could see that Severn was ill. His lodgings were destroyed and he had no place to stay. The kindly Clarks offered him a room at their apartments until he could make a more permanent arrangement.

Severn's painting 'The Death of Alcibiades' remained unfinished. He had left it untouched as Keats went into the final weeks of his illness. He was well aware that in spite of feeling unwell it had to be finished in time for the Academy Exhibition.

William Ewing, the sculptor, gave him the use of part of his studio, and he managed to complete the work over the next month. The picture was a success; the Academy funded an amount to cover his expenses in Rome and awarded him a further £130.

Joseph Severn enjoyed a long life, spending many years in Italy. By nothing short of a miracle he escaped the consumption; a disease contracted by contact with someone suffering from it. Whilst caring for Keats over the months he must have taken in the germ many times over.

As the year passed, Severn lived with his memories of Keats. To pass through the Piazza di Spagna was always painful for him. At times in the year after the poet's death he could often be found within the Protestant Cemetery, standing at the foot of Keats' grave. As summer came, red-rimmed daisies covered the grave over. And soon flowers of blue violets began to find their way amongst the daisies. When Severn returned again to Rome after being in England for almost twenty years, he first went to the grave. The cemetery's gardener complained that he could not keep the violets on the grave; because every visitor picked them as a memento of their pilgrimage. Severn was delighted to hear of it; "Sow and plant twice as much," he smiled.

After two years, the poet's friends had still to agree on a final headstone inscription. Though Severn had designed an emblem, a lyre with half its strings broken. At first he claimed that it was Keats' idea, but later admitted that it was his own. The lyre emblem was quickly agreed. However Keats' executors were opposed on the matter of the inscription. Taylor and Hessey, wished only for the words that Keats had asked for. "Here lies one whose name was writ in water." Charles Brown disagreed, saying there must be more to it! It wasn't until Brown's arrival in Italy in the autumn of 1822 that the inscription that is on the stone today was agreed and these words were cut:

> "This grave contains all that was Mortal, of a YOUNG ENGLISH POET Who, on his Death Bed, in the Bitterness of his Heart at the Malicious Power of his Enemies, desired these Words to be engraven on his Tomb Stone."

One can only guess at what Keats' reaction would have been had he known of this strange inscription. He would have most probably rubbed it out, with; "This has nothing to do with me, I was ill at the time." (As he did write against a prologue that his publisher wrote in one of his books of poetry.)

Sixty-one years after Keats' death, Joseph Severn's body was laid to rest at his friend's left hand. His gravestone stands proudly beside that of Keats. Nearby another memorial can be found, and there lies the heart of another great English poet, Percy Bysshe Shelley, who also died young – one year later than Keats.

Oh, how the ghostly poetry must echo around that far-off foreign field.

APPENDIX
Joseph Severn and the Funeral of Shelley

After Shelley's death from drowning whilst sailing from Leghorn to Spezia in July 1822, he was cremated on a funeral pyre at Pisa. At the cremation were Lord Byron, Leigh Hunt and Edward Trelawny. As the driftwood fire burned on the beach, Hunt threw the book of Keats' poems found on Shelley's body into the flames, and a reckless Trelawny thrust his hand into the heat and retrieved the heart. (It was recorded that he carried the scars on his hand for many years.)

The remains and ashes were placed in a casket which Mary Shelley took charge of. Later she decided that the casket should be placed with their son William 'Willmouse' who had been buried in the "parte antica" of the Testaccio cemetery three years earlier. Shelley's ashes, in the oak casket, were sent to Mr Freeborn, the British Consul in Rome. But by the time they arrived, the Rome authorities had banned further internments in the "parte antica". Mary Shelley's wishes could not be carried out, and the casket was placed in the consulate wine cellar until other arrangements could be made.

Mary, still at Genoa and unable to go to Rome asked Joseph Severn for assistance. On December the 16th 1822, Leigh Hunt wrote, "You have nothing, dear Severn, but funeral tasks put upon you, but they are for extraordinary people and excellent friends." Trelawny also said that he would go to Rome in February 1823 to help with the problem.

Mr Freeborn the Consul and Joseph Severn, having both tried without success to get permission for the burial, decided to ask for permission to exhume the body of William and rebury it together with his father's ashes in a new enclosure. Permission was granted, and the funeral was scheduled for January 23rd. What came about is best described by the contents of a letter written by Severn that same day:

"I have just returned from the funeral of poor Shelley. Our plan was frustrated, after I had got a permission to disinter the bones of the child for, on opening the grave we discovered a skeleton 5½" feet. Yet it appeared to be under the stone, so that some mistake must have been made in placing the stone. To search further we dare not, for it was in the presence of many respectful but wondering Italians; nay, I thought it would have been a doubtful and horrible thing to disturb any more strangers' graves in a foreign land. So we proceeded very respectfully to deposit poor Shelley's ashes alone. There were present General Cockburn, Sir Charles Sykes, Messrs Kirkup, Westmacott, Scoles, Freeborn, and the Revs. W, Cook and Burgess. These two gentlemen, with myself, wished it to be done solemnly and decently. So the box was enclosed in a coffin, and it was done altogether as by the hands of friends."

A few weeks later Trelawny came to Rome. He did not like the position of Shelley's grave among a number of others, and he purchased what seemed to him a better plot near the old wall. No problems arose over the exhumation, and the ashes were transferred to their present resting place.

Percy Bysshe Shelley's tombstone can still be seen in the "parte antica" Protestant cemetery, not so far from those of Keats and Severn.

The true site of the grave of Shelley's son William remains a mystery.

PART IV

Doctor James Clark
1788–1870
(later Sir James Clark)

Born on the 14th of December 1788 at Cullen in the county of Banff, his early education was conducted at a small church school in Fordyce, after which he studied in college at Aberdeen. There he studied art and the law. Towards the end of his schooldays he changed direction, going on to take up medicine at the College of Surgeons in Edinburgh. Passing out as a doctor, a youthful Clark became an assistant surgeon in the navy, and served aboard the *Thistle*. He survived a wreck off New Jersey, after which he returned to Edinburgh to continue with his studies, receiving his MD in 1817.

In 1818 he obtained a commission as doctor to a gentleman suffering advanced consumption, who he accompanied to the south of France. His patient died, and from then on Clark became interested in the effects of climate on disease.

In 1819 he settled in Rome where he married, and became a well-known physician to the English colony there.

In his treatments Clark used the methods of the day, the letting of blood, and fasting almost to the point of starvation.

If he had access to one, he might have used the new 'stethoscope', the French invention, that was just coming into use in London at about the time that Keats was in Italy. However, for reasons best known only to himself, he diagnosed Keats' problem to be with his stomach and the state of his mind, and said that there was little wrong with his lungs. When after Keats' death an autopsy was carried out by Clark and an Italian doctor, they found his lungs were almost entirely destroyed, Clark then remarked that it was surprising that his patient had survived for so long in such a dire condition.

In 1826 Clark returned to England, and settled in London. He published a number of papers, including one on Pulmonary Consumption, and was admitted to the Licentiate of the College of Physicians.

Appointed physician to Queen Victoria in 1837, he became a firm friend of Prince Albert, was awarded the F.R.S and eventually Knighted.

A problem diagnosis brought him a great deal of criticism – the affair of one of the Queen's Ladies-in-Waiting, Lady Flora Hastings. Lady Flora's abdomen became visibly swollen, and the court gossips assumed pregnancy. Clark's diagnosis was said to have leant in that direction. But in truth no examination of the lady was carried out by him, he only gave advice and council. Unfortunately Lady Flora died, and was later found to have a large abdominal tumour. Shock ran through the establishment at the loss of a Lady well loved by the Queen, and a popular member at court. Clark received most of the blame, and was brought to a court of enquiry. He sacrificed himself for the mistakes of others, and bore the trial without complaint which afterwards he said had almost killed him. It seems that all Sir James did was to suggest to the suffering woman that, to silence the rumours flying around the court, she submit herself to a medical examination which would discover the cause of her condition. Apparently she refused.

Clark retained his position at court, and was often seen at the medical section of the University of London, which owes something to his work. He is also known to have supported William Farr's work on mathematics when applied to medicine.

He died aged eighty-one, and is remembered mostly for his treatment of John Keats.

Epilogue on a Shortened Life

The news of Keats' death took three weeks to reach his friends in England. Since he had left them they had put pens to paper, saying how much they feared that which seemed to be the inevitable. Brown wore an air of false good humour, and raged about the poet's brother George. The publishers, Taylor and Hessey recommended recourse to religion. Leigh Hunt, the confirmed atheist, wrote to Joseph Severn; "Tell him, he is only before us on the road, as he was in everything else."

Fanny Brawne, who had nursed him during his last two months at Wentworth Place, seemed prepared to face up to the truth. She confided in her mother, "I believe he must soon die, when you hear of his death tell me immediately, I am not a fool!" Writing to Keats' sister she told her, "I shall never see him again."

When Brown broke the news of Keats' death at Wentworth Place, he said that he was amazed at Fanny's firmness of mind. Yet this apparent 'firmness of mind' was false, for she was deeply affected by her loss. The next day she prepared to mourn, donning black, cutting her long hair short. She could be found wandering aimlessly about the heath, or reading over and over his letters alone in her room.

In his letter to Severn, Brown wrote, "It is now five days since she heard it. I shall not speak of the first shock, nor of the following days, it is enough she is now pretty well and thro'out she has shown a firmness of mind which I little expected from one so young, and under such a load of grief."

It would be the 27 March before she summoned the strength to express her grief in a letter to Keats' sister Fanny:

You will forgive me. I am sure, my dear Fanny, that I did not write to you before. I could not for my own sake and I would not for yours, as it was better you should be prepared for what, even knowing as much as you did, you could not expect. I should like to hear that you my dearest Sister are well, for myself, I am patient resigned, very resigned. I know my Keats is happy, happier a thousand times that he could have been here, for Fanny, you do not, you never can know how much he has suffered. So much that I do believe, were it in my power I would not bring him back. All that grieves me now is that I was not with him, and so near it as I was. Some day my dear girl I will tell you the reason and give you additional cause to hate those who should have been his friends. And yet it was a great deal through his kindness for me for he foresaw what would happen, he at least was never deceived about his complaint, though the Doctors were ignorant and unfeeling enough to send him to that wretched country to die, for it is now known that his recovery was impossible before he left us, and he might have died here with so many friends to soothe him and me, me with him. All we have to console ourselves with is the great joy he felt that all his misfortunes were at an end. At the very last he said 'I am dying thank God the time is come,' and in a letter from Mr Severn written about a fortnight before he died and which was not shown to me, so that I thought he would live months at least, if he did not recover, he says 'he is still alive and calm, If I say more it will be too much, yet at times I have thought him better but he would not hear of it, the thought of recovery is beyond every thing dreadful to him – we now dare not perceive any improvement for the hope of death seems his only comfort, he talks of the quiet grave as the first rest he can ever have' – In that letter he mentions that he had given directions

166

how he would be buried, the purse you sent him and your last letter (which he never read, for he would never open either your letters or mine after he left England) with some hair, I believe of mine, he desired to be placed in his coffin. The truth is I cannot very well go on at present with this, another time I will tell you more. [The letter continued about the affairs of Fanny Keats' guardian who kept the girl close and restricted; Keats himself had many a dispute with Richard Abbey on the same subject.]

In another letter dated, Hampstead May 23, 1821. Fanny Brawne reveals to Fanny Keats her feelings for her brother. The letter begins with mundane things before she says:

I have half filled this letter without a word of what I intended. I have not mentioned your brother. To no one but you would I mention him. I will suffer no one but you to speak to me of him. They are too uninterested in him to have any right to mention what is to you and me, so great a loss. I have copied a letter from Mr Severn giving an account of the last days of his life. No one knows I have it but you, and I had not sealed it up, as I thought you might wish to see it, but if you do, you must prepare for great pain, if you would rather not make yourself again unhappy, do not read it, I think you will be wise. It took me a long time to write. I have not looked at it since, nor do I mean to do so at present, but I mention it to you because though it gives pain, it also gives a certain kind of pleasure in letting us know how glad he was to die at last. Dear Fanny, no one but you can feel with me – All his friends have forgotten him, they have got over the first shock, and that with them is all. [Fanny Brawne could not have been more wrong, they had not forgotten him! Some of his closest friends worked to promote his name for many years after his death. Fanny had always been out of touch with his friends, most of them didn't like her and the feeling was mutual.] They think I have done the same, which I do not wonder at, for I have taken care never to trouble them with any feelings of mine, but I can tell you who next to me (I must say next to me) loved him best, that I have not got over it and never shall – It's better for me that I should not forget him but not for you, you have other things to look forward to – and I would not have said any thing about him for I was affraid of distressing you but I did not like to write to you without telling you how I felt about him and leaving it to you whether the subject should be mentioned in our letters – In a letter you sent me some time ago you mentioned your brother George in a manner that made me think you had been mislead about him. He is no favorite of mine and he never liked me so that I am not likely to say too much in his favor from affection for him. But I must say I think he is more blamed than he should be. I think him extravagant and selfish but people in their great zeal make him out much worse than that – Soon after your brother Tom died, my dear John wrote to him offering him any assistance or money in his power. At that time he was not engaged to me and having just lost one brother felt all his affection turned towards the one remained – George I dare say at first had no thoughts of accepting his offers but when his affairs did not succeed and he had a wife and one child to support, with the prospect of another, I cannot wonder that he should consider them first and as he could not get what he wanted without coming to England he unfortunately came – By that time your brother wished to marry himself, but he could not refuse the money. It may appear very bad in George to leave him 60 pounds when he owed 80, but he had many reasons to suppose the inconvenience would not last long.

Fanny Brawne reveals her engagement to Keats for the first time. As for marriage it wasn't set in stone as far as the poet was concerned. She carries on with the letter, warning Keats' sister to be on her guard against George as far as the money of her inheritance was concerned.

The letter that Fanny copied out in part for Fanny Keats was from the original written to John Taylor by Joseph Severn, dated 16 April 1821. The excerpt is as follows:

Four days previous to his death – the change was so great that I passed each moment in dread, not knowing what the next would have – he was calm and firm at its approaches to a most astonishing degree. He told me not to tremble for he did not think that he should be convulsed; he said "did you ever see any one die?" "no" "well I pity you, poor Severn. What trouble and danger you have got into for me – now you must be firm for it will not last long. I shall soon be laid in the quiet grave – O! I can feel the cold earth upon me – The daisies growing over me – O for this quiet – it will be my first" – When the morning light came and still found him alive how bitterly he grieved – I cannot bear his cries – Each day he would look up in the Doctor's face to discover how long he should live he would say "how long will this posthumous life of mine last" that look was more than we could ever bear. The extreme brightness of his eyes with his poor pallid face were not earthly. These four nights I watched him, each night expecting his death – on the 5th day the Doctor prepared me for it. At 4 o'clock in the afternoon the poor fellow bade me lift him up in bed, he breathed with great difficulty and seemed to lose the power of coughing up the phlegm, an intense sweat came over him so that my breath felt cold to him. "Don't breathe on me it comes like ice" he clasped my hand very fast as I held him in my arms. The phlegm rattled in his throat, it increased but still he seemed without pain, he looked upon me with extreme sensibility but without pain, at 11 he died in my arms.

This excerpt was part of a longer letter, and was marked 'Sheet 2, from Mr Severn April 16th'. This is the letter that John Taylor, Keats' publisher passed to Isabella Jones, the beautiful socialite with whom Keats and himself had been romantically attached. She was most scathing about it; saying to Taylor, "such sickening sentimentality."

As time moved on and truth became mixed with myth and legend, the friendships which had held during the poet's lifetime fractured. Letters were either destroyed or suppressed, and material which would have proved invaluable was lost to us. Dilke's grandson, Sir Charles, set about finding all of Fanny Brawne's letters to Keats, finally burning them in the grate of his parlour. So successful was he in his endeavour that not one has since come to light.

Brown fell out with Taylor and Hessey over a proposed biography of the poet. Leigh Hunt was criticised by all for his betrayal of Keats in his *Byron and his contemporaries* published in 1828, in which he gave Keats a weakness of character. Benjamin Haydon fell out with Hunt over the non-return of borrowed cutlery. Charles Wentworth Dilke wrote Charles Armitage-Brown a vitriolic letter supporting George Keats over what Brown had accused him of. And so it went on, it seemed that whatever spell Keats had cast had finally been broken.

Keats' poems mentioned or quoted from

Imitation of Spenser. (1813)

Written on the day that Mr Leigh Hunt left Prison. (Feb, 1815)

O' Solitude! If I must with Thee Dwell. (Nov, 1815)

How many Bards Gild the lapses of Time. (March, 1816)

Epistle to Charles Cowden Clarke. (Sept, 1816)

On first looking into Chapman's Homer. (Oct, 1816)

I Stood Tip-Toe Upon a Little Hill. (Dec, 1816)

Sonnet Written at the end of 'The Floure and The Lefe'. (Feb, 1817)

Endymion. (April-Dec, 1817)

Meg Merrilies. (July, 1818)

The Eve of St Agnes. (Feb, 1819)

The Eve of St Mark. (Unfinished) – (Feb, 1819)

La Belle Dame sans Merci. (April, 1819)

Bright Star. (First version) – (April, 1819)

Bright Star (Final version) – (Sep, 1820)

The Sonnet to Sleep. (April, 1819)

Ode to Psyche. (April, 1819)

On Charles Armitage Brown. (April, 1819)

Ode on a Grecian Urn. (May, 1819)

Ode to a Nightingale. (May, 1819)

Otho the Great. (A play) (June-Aug, 1819)

Lamia. (July-Aug, 1819)

Hyperion. (Aug-Sept, 1819)

King Stephen. (Nov, 1819)

Keats' Sonnet – When I Have Fears.

January 1818.

When I have fears that I may cease to be
Before my pen has glean'd my teeming brain,
Before high piled books, in charact'ry
Hold like rich garners the full ripen'd grain;
When I behold, upon the night's starr'd face,
Huge cloudy symbols of a high romance,
And think that I may never live to trace
Their shadows, with the magic hand of chance;
And when I feel, fair creature of an hour!
That I shall never look upon thee more,
Never have relish in the faery power
Of unreflecting love! then on the shore
Of the wide world I stand alone, and think,
Till love and fame to nothingness do sink.